IF ONLY

TERRY WEST

A Wild Wolf Publication

Published by Wild Wolf Publishing in 2018

Copyright © 2018 Terry West

First print

ISBN: 978-1-907954-72-6
Also available in e-book

www.wildwolfpublishing.com

Acknowledgments

I would like to say thank you to my wonderful family, especially my wife, Linda, for being by my side through all my trials. I really am not sure if I would still be here if it wasn't for her.

Equally, I owe a huge amount of gratitude to my daughter, Charlene, who has experienced most of the tragedies in my life, offering unconditional love and support throughout, despite her own traumas. Without her, I could not have written this book.

To all my friends, past and present, including Terry Kilbride, who have stood alongside me for the last fifty-plus years – thank you.

Kind thoughts also to Rod Glenn at Wild Wolf publishing for taking a chance on this book and to researcher John Iley for all the extra bits – some of which we did not even know until we came to put the words down.

Finally, to Tony Horne, my ghost-writer, who has been so patient and passionate about my story, thank you for believing in what I had to write. He specialises in this kind of book so I recommend you look him up if you find yourself with your own story to tell.

His website is www.tonyhornebooks.com

And to you, thank you for reading.

Prologue

Tuesday 15 August 2017

I don't know why I am here. I have rarely courted the media. Mum and Terry Kilbride took that on – an unstoppable machine that they fought, spent years correcting and finally when they had the strength, attempting to shape their own agenda.

Mum is not here anymore. Terry keeps fighting. Ian Brady's death in May 2017 has opened a new can of worms. It brings it all back. None of it really went away.

I have a choice. Do I shun the circus or join its merry dance? For years, this story has been a currency that fuels newspaper sales and fills TV airtime. And that's what they called it; a story. Today, they would call it a 'journey'.

I can tell you, I am now in my late 60s and this is neither a journey nor a story. It is real life. My life. And of course, those who walked into it, preceded me and will still pick up the pieces after I am gone.

I don't know why I am here.

I am invited to participate in a TV show. I am not media friendly. I say little. I lock it all in. It plays in my mind over and over, but I can't find the words. It is a silent movie. For most people, it is simply that three months have passed and the producers are probably thinking they will sell this for the first anniversary of his death. They come in at this point. They join the 'story' now.

But I have lived with it. For a very long time. It has defined my life. The choices I have made and the decisions I have taken all fundamentally stem from the day my choice was to make the wrong decision.

And now I *am* talking about it.

I don't know why I am here. Today, they would call it Post Traumatic Stress Disorder and there is counselling available. In 1964, they did not have such a name nor help. I was just a fourteen-year-old boy who did not go to the fair with his sister. In 2017, that post-traumatic stress is the only constant I have known in my life. I live with it still and it is the norm.

I see today as I see every day and every day is *that* day.

I do know why I am here. Maybe I realise that my own time is running out and that, as horrific as the crimes committed were, other atrocities are sadly more front of mind now. I feel too, that, if somebody helps me offload even if coerced through the medium of a TV debate then I will take that.

I have it here locked in my heart and my head and always will do. I am not used to exposure, and apart from Mum, nobody has really ever got under my skin about the effects of that day. I do not feel safe here on recorded television, but Terry Kilbride gives me confidence. Once I get over the dynamics of the medium, I realise I have nothing to lose. There is, after all, no moral high ground for an opposing point of view to assume – as is often the way with these set-up jobs. You can't put anybody up with a different opinion and expect the public to side with them in a case such of ours. As media-unsavvy as I was, I got that at least.

Naïve perhaps, I had not legislated for the unknown. I am in the Green Room waiting when Bernard comes over to me and says he saw them at the fair. I knew Bernard before this happened and I have known him on and off since. But I have never heard him say this before.

'I used to go to school with your Les,' he told me.

I stare him blankly in the face. I only knew him as a good footballer. I didn't for one moment realise that in fact they knew each other. And I only find out a quarter of a century later.

He tells me of two mutual acquaintances who also played football. Some had been in the same class at Miles Platting just under a couple of miles outside Manchester City centre and I did not even know. I had no idea he would be on this show. I assumed it was for family members, but his knowledge reminded me he was genuine. It also of course flagged up that there were people in our Lesley's world who were not in mine. I thought I knew my kid sister inside out and I never had considered her sphere of influence or those who had brushed past the family and had their own story to tell.

Enter Tommy Rhattigan. I had learned he had published a book called *A Slice of Bread and Jam,* but apart from that I had never heard of him. This also contributed to my fear as to why I was here. I meet a Gorton priest too who claimed he had a narrow escape. There were enough people immediate to the 'story' who could produce hours of footage to add to those that already existed. I was sure that we didn't need any 'hangers on'.

I understood that 'near-misses' painted a picture for the police especially and I realised, of course, that with any serial criminal, there would be people who with time felt they had been close but had somehow escaped. Half a century later what was the point in them airing in the same documentary as those who had lost and been scarred for life?

I did not doubt the sincerity of these individuals, but I was also aware that people liked to dine out on anecdotes. I was acutely conscious too that some serial killers attracted fantasists. This would come to haunt the family in time. In time I see him on *Loose Women* on ITV, and hear my words that I speak on this documentary being said by him, as if they were his own. My eldest refused to watch.

I am still nervous after the filming. Bernard tells me that he had four sisters and would feel exactly as I did. Suddenly I begin to open up to him and start to say things that stop me in my tracks, because I know I do not open up like this. The meeting of the eras does this. I feel a connection with Bernard because of his to Lesley. It is a long time since I have met someone outside of the family who has wandered back into my life and can give me this perspective. We hug. I don't do hugs.

Tommy Rhattigan announces that nobody should leave. He has something for us. He produces copies of his book for each of us. He seems a decent enough person, but it just goes to show that however sensitive, or well-meaning you are, only very few have lived this story. Others have dipped in and out it and have different reasons for being here. The point is that you either carry this around every hour of every day or you don't.

Across the room, I see Terry who is here because he is often so. For the families, he more than anyone had worked the media since Mum died. Often the choice was simple: if you participate you at least have a say. If you don't, they can run what they like. It was unthinkable to think they could ever air any show without one of us participating, but every single time required the maximum effort to relive just the minimum of the pain and accommodate the needs of the media.

And even then you could only give them a snapshot. The experience has scrambled my mind – a mixture of having so much to say, but being unable to express it and certainly not within the constraints of a time-restricted TV programme. Yet, for the first time a real desire to attempt to put down on a paper what I saw and felt, what I lived through and which parts of life passed me by – all of course with the knowledge that I still retain the gift of life, something which was taken away from my beautiful little sister.

I know why I am here. For the first time, it is right to tell *my* story.

Chapter 1 – Christmas Day, 1964

I was fourteen years old. My brothers Tommy and Brett were eight and four. Lesley Ann came in between at ten. My mum Ann *Downey* worked in the canteen at Express Newspapers; my father, Terry Downey, was an engineer near Trafford Park, Manchester. Alan, a long-distance lorry driver lived with Mum and us kids when he wasn't on the road at our maisonette in Charnley Walk, off Varley Street near Ancoats.

For once, the previous six months had been the calmest, more stable that any of us had known. Life consisted of lots of family trips to Wales or maybe Scotland in the back of Alan's van, with all the sofa beds he was meant to be delivering, each of us always winding each other up every single day, followed by endless trips to the chip shop at night for the scrapings.

Our lot was simple and we were broke, but we had finally stopped being shunted from one council house to another, often squatting – at one point for several months in an empty house. Mum would go into the housing office and pull some sort of stunt and we were moving again, always climbing some sort of housing ladder. She had been self sufficient all her life, and in this it showed, barely knowing her own father, who became a Prisoner of War in Germany – and now divorced herself, for a couple of years.

But it was Alan's arrival that brought her happiness after splitting from my birth Dad. They had met by chance in the pub. She seemed genuinely happy for the first time I could remember. He shifted furniture around the country and everyone in the family remembers how he once sent a telegram from Leek in Staffordshire to say he was on his way to ours!

After years of struggle, surviving day to day without real prospects and living off scraps, we at least had stability. It was a different era. You didn't fret about work. There was lots of it – from apprenticeships to jobs for life. You didn't worry about leaving school with nothing. Of course, all the lads wanted to be footballers. Everybody dreamed of being George Best, but when that idea crashed you knew that you would get paid enough to manage on by the end of the week, in whatever path you followed. As soon as you could get out of school, you did. There was little long-term strategy like university. You lived on hand-me-downs, leftovers and shared bathwater. There was the radio and a little television. You might have a car if you were lucky. You could play out in the street with no fear and be home for dark. Les loved her roller-skates and Rebel, the family dog. The summers were longer and hotter – possibly. You knew the name of your next-door neighbour and Sundays were sacred. We were happy. We had nothing, but we had each other.

Part of that home life meant Sunday School. My sister Lesley was always there – the apple in Mum's eye, nurturing this little girl into this beautiful young lady. Quite loveable, she would do anything for you and thrived in that sense of belonging that the church brought, and even though my Mum went on to have a love-hate relationship with religion for obvious reasons, there was no doubt that Sundays were special and the community came together. It was unthinkable to miss service and people would hang around forever afterwards. Everybody had time that they do not today and that facilitated the endless but fearless playing out. Lesley, at ten, was just like every other child at that age and you thought nothing of it.

There had not been a story in Great Britain like the one she was tragically about to walk into; nor were the modern-day distractions and non-stop news to report it. You felt safe, and even though there were some bad types about, largely, you *were* safe.

If you asked me what Lesley would have become in life, I have no idea. It was way too early to know her ambitions. She was just living and loving life – happy just being, which even today seems hard to achieve. That innocence that she was robbed of is often lost nowadays anyway because of *life*.

My little sis always had friends around. With her curly hair, she was shy but gaining confidence all the time, and from a very early age, had a strong sense of right and wrong, more so than any child I had met. She got this from Mum of course, and that very value at such a young age naturally makes her fate even worse – at the hands of people who had no boundaries.

Occasionally, she would have a little cob on – perhaps as a result of being sandwiched in amongst her three brothers – and she always had an air of mischief about her. If I brought a girlfriend home, she would remain seated at the top of the stairs having a nose.

But she was happy and beautiful. Together, Christmas Day 1964 could not have been more perfect. In our world, we had arrived. In your world, there may seem nothing to be envious of. Five of us were living in a two bedroomed council house, from which we were not about to be moved on anytime soon, and this year we had a tree bigger than we had ever had before.

It had stood tall all week in the run up to the big day. It represented so much more than Christmas. It stood for peace in our family. We would never have money. We couldn't even spell materialism. It didn't matter. Christmas Day 1964 glowed and as dawn broke on that morning, you would not find a happier household.

Mum had an early sherry. The TV was on in the background, from early morning Christmas Services to Leslie Crowther and Julie Andrews, to documentaries on the Great War and Billy Smart's Circus, and by evening, *Christmas With The Stars,* with Roy Castle, Benny Hill, Billy Cotton, Dick Emery and *The Black and White Minstrels.*

The atmosphere in the house was crazy – a frenzy of excitement. Everyone was a child. Even the children! Mum was so relaxed, happy that Alan had come up from London. It stands as a moment in time.

When it came to open the presents, Lesley received a sewing machine; Tommy got a record player. I don't even remember what I found under the tree. I was coming down with a heavy cough and cold, and with it, fell a curtain in our lives that defines us all ever since.

It was a perfect day, but very soon it was to become the last one. The saddest of days was about to begin. And from that moment, all the days rolled into one.

It stands as a moment in time because it is the only marker to before and after. Time was about to stop.

Forever.

Chapter 2 – Boxing Day, 1964

The fire was on, mince pies were in the oven again, and *White Christmas* was on the telly. Again. Boxing Day afternoon always meant football or the Silcock Wonder Fair in Ancoats. It had never been any different, and despite us moving around, Hulme Hall Lane Red Rec was a fixture in the calendar. Just a stone's throw from my school, it had rolled into town for as long as I could remember. After largely home-based family festivities, everyone I knew looked forward to getting out around teatime on the day after Christmas and meeting up the fair. If it turned up today, people would probably snub it. But it looked massive back then. Waltzers, dodgems, Coconut Shy, and Win A Goldfish were standard. They had everyone eating out of their hand.

Except me on that day. For the first time in years, it didn't look like I would be going. That Christmas Day flu lingered and, as the sniffles wore on, I told Lesley that if I was any better I would take her, but I really could not face going out. My nose was runny and my legs were heavy. I just wanted to stay in, be warm and give it a miss this year. There would be other Christmases and other fairs.

Except there were to be no more.

Lesley left without me. In her blue coat and red shoes.

'Enjoy yourself,' I said as she parted. 'I'm sorry I can't come'.

'Don't worry, I understand,' she replied.

These were the last words I spoke to her and she to me. This was the final time I saw her.

The fair was ten minutes away. I shut the door and thought nothing more of it.

I went to bed just glad she was going to go with a friend.

If I could turn back the clock, I would have wrapped up warm and found a way to go for an hour. As poorly as I felt, I so wish I could have summoned up the strength, got dressed and just got through it.

I have replayed this moment to eternity.

Instead, Tommy and Lesley left together and my little sister went to Mrs Clark's, a neighbour of my Mum's.

Lesley was due home for tea at 5pm. No more than an hour, Mum had said, as she had done so many times. She never made it back.

Tommy had come back to the house before home time. I remember him having that red-cheeked winter look of warmth, but clearly cold – the type where you talk and see your breath in front of you. He was confused as to why he was not the last one in.

He had last seen Lesley on The Wall of Death and had assumed she had gone on ahead of him. He returned alone. Mum and Alan had been preparing snowballs outside for the idyllic Christmas scene. I had finally succumbed and, as I hit the pillow, I did not know at first that Lesley had not come home.

Ahead, lay only the nightmare.

Tommy froze as Mum and Alan looked at each other. Surely there was an innocent explanation. The first obvious port of call was downstairs to Mrs Clark's. She was clearly there with her daughter, Linda. I was in a half sleep as my brother slammed the door on his way out and Mum momentarily carried on beavering about, carrying on as normal, still expecting relatives to turn up. That's how it was in an extended family. Buses would run infrequently and unpredictably. Aunties and Uncles would arrive when they did, and there would always be a brew on and something in the oven. Lesley, in particular was very fond of Auntie Elsie. She would race home to see her. We were waiting on both.

But she hadn't. Tommy rushed back in, a good quarter of an hour later – perhaps it was longer. It seemed an eternity. He was out of breath and broke the news to the family that Mrs Clark *hadn't* gone to the fair.

'What?' someone exclaimed after a jaw-dropping silence.

We all stopped. Froze. Then went into overdrive.

None of us had ever been late except for Tommy once, when he had been playing out roller-skating. The rollicking he received ensured we would never run that risk again – even on Boxing Day.

By this point, I am off the couch and at the entrance to the kitchen. I am white-faced from my fever. I am shaking inside. The illness and panic met each other half way so I could not really differentiate. My younger brother was the messenger. It should have been me. Except there shouldn't have been a messenger. Even at this early stage, I feared the worst. But I couldn't say it out loud. I was mute, tongue-tied, transfixed like a statue in fear. And there was a hierarchy to respect in our house. Mum and Alan called the tune.

Tommy managed to blurt it out. Mrs Clark was tired and didn't feel like going. Linda and Lesley had gone alone. Normally, you wouldn't think too much of that in 1964. But now, with no Lesley, it consumed our thoughts.

Tommy explained why he had been so long. He had run all the way back to the fair in the dark of night, guided only by street lights and the tacky signs of the fair. It was the coldest, blackest time of the year – always dark by half past three.

I was shivering – Mum urging me towards the fire. Nothing could warm my heart.

Mum's contentment was now at the brink of despair. Back then, home time meant home time and you would give a child a few minutes and, on Boxing Day, perhaps a few minutes more. You wouldn't want to be anything other than relaxed at Christmas, but soon five minutes became ten, and then an hour has passed and you start roaming the streets, calling Lesley's name, all the time wondering if she has gone back whilst you are searching.

Mum and Alan began an agonising few hours. It was the night that never ended. Across the street, decorations shone forth from faceless council flats that at no other time of year came to life. Their joy clung to the spirit of the season. Ours was drowning in the distant drone of the fair. We didn't see those lights any more. Ours were going out fast.

They made for Lesley's school friends' houses. Everybody lived within a few doors of each other back then. Mum told me that when she went up a garden path, her heart missed a beat with hope as she knocked on the door, only for it to skip a second time and race at twice the speed as the answer kept coming back as no. Lesley was not at any of her mates' houses.

Of course, all roads led back to the Rec. Spinning before Mum and Alan were hundreds of people oblivious to atrocity and on this of all days. The hope that knocking on individual doors gave so many times in such quick succession, and the comfort that Mum knew those people was dashed as she walked onto the field – a sea of fun and laughter and so many people she *didn't* know. Something that had always been part of our Christmas now took her out of her comfort zone, approaching complete strangers, asking if they had seen this little girl in a blue coat 'about this high, maybe an hour before'.

I can't say that people did not want to know, but if they hadn't spotted Lesley then they just wanted to get on the next ride. It was Boxing Day after all.

I waited and waited for Mum and Alan to come home. As I sat there, I didn't hear the Christmas music. I couldn't tell you what was on the TV now. I was cold from the warmest of fires. In short, I was terrified and my parents' return just made it worse. I looked at them hopefully, on the brink of tears. They said nothing and nor did I.

It was the silence that spoke volumes.

I ran upstairs to my room sobbing my heart out. I knew. I just knew.

Mum and Alan tore downstairs and *tore* into Mrs Clark. Linda was there but no Lesley. I couldn't understand it. They had got separated and she had come home alone. I am sure the whole neighbourhood heard Mum's wrath. She was now in overdrive and had to be restrained by Alan. Looking for blame got confused with looking for Lesley.

Each false lead and every cry of dismay got us nowhere. They ate up valuable minutes and we were running that gauntlet again of time stopping and then going at twice the speed. For all the hours that we knew nothing, it lurked in the subconscious that Our Les would just turn up. Yet, also you could rant and rave at Mrs Clark, but you would have to cut it short because the voice in your head said that you were wasting time and running out of it. Lesley was out there and we had to find her tonight.

I couldn't stay inside any longer. If only I had found this physical strength earlier, none of us would be in this position. My mind had left my body. The aches and pains of flu were nothing now compared to how my heart was being ripped apart. To be full of cold, and yet immune to the crackles of the fire, meant that my sensitivities had left me. Numb in all ways possible, I begged Mum to let me look with her and Alan. Her instincts were utterly torn. We needed to cling. It was time to stay together. Even though we were ripped apart.

I grabbed Mum's arm. There was no second movement. We locked together. Adult holding child. Child holding adult. My tears imprisoned inside. They can't get out. And if they rolled down my cheek they would have fallen like icicles. I wouldn't have known. I just held Mum and wanted it over. I said nothing. The words were incarcerated too. I was trapped in my soul.

Mum could see it and knew even at this early stage that I was consumed with guilt. I was beyond panic. She told me not to blame myself, even though nobody had said as such. Maternal instinct had kicked in. I had none. Not a drop of it. No hunch. Just certainty. Just cold hard facts. Lesley was gone. It was my fault.

Mum hugged me without words. That told me I was to blame, but she was not blaming me.

We made for the fair again. It is what you did. You retraced her steps. With blind hope and a permanent sinking feeling. Mum shouted Lesley's name, occasionally spotting what she thought was a blue coat.

There were now a few of us. Word had spread and we split up, with some people going to check the stream and the derelict mill nearby, which felt more haunted than ever. As I clung to Mum's arms, I knew that the river conjured a bad gut feeling, but also that we had to cover all bases. Mum was just adamant that we didn't stand still. We had to scour every blade of grass however long the night lasted. The funfair all around me was a blurred headlight in the distance. The screams of terror on The Wall of Death resonated throughout the Rec. Our own walls were coming crashing down, yet nobody could hear our wails of pain. Nor, more importantly, Lesley's.

Chapter 3 – Boxing Day Night, 1964

By the stream, Mum could hear Chris Montez *Let's Dance* from the fair. Lesley loved that song. Mum thought it might be a sign. I realised already by this point that you clung to anything. Any song. Any clue.

It was neither. It was an emotion. A reaction. A desperation. The first of many.

We headed home and I flung the door open, searching through the maisonette, shouting Lesley's name at every twist and turn. Then, nobody said anything.

What was there to say?

I could see Mum talking to Alan and they clearly looked as though they had made a decision. They did not want to stand still and settled us all down, turning their backs once again to walk the streets. This time, they were not chasing the lights, sounds and smells of the fairground. They knew it was serious. They were walking to the nearest police station at Mill Street. Lesley could have been dead by now.

We were all frightened – and I mean terrified in a way that few people experience in life. Even Mum, and I suspect an outwardly calm Alan too. Most people experience fear at some points in their life, but it usually subsides. This was an uncontrollable panic cast across every one of us, regardless of age and life experience. The stillness of the Christmas night and the emptiness of the roads with so little traffic, and almost no public transport, echoed that hollow emotion. It was beyond late, and therefore, hope as well, and as it seemed initially at the police station, reason too.

Mum was pretty much dismissed by the front desk, suggesting that these things happen and they might want to give it another hour or so. When Mum said Lesley had been to the fair, he barely stirred as though he had heard it all before. I do not know the name of the police officer and I doubt now that he could have changed history, but I am sure he has had plenty of time to reflect on his indifference that night.

He, of course, picked the wrong person to agitate. Mum was furious as he rejected her, on one hand, with the 'kids coming home late all the time' line, and on the other, with Christmas leave meaning staff were few and far between.

On Alan's intervention they compromised with an unhappy standoff, notionally taking their bare details and offering 11 pm as a time when he might seriously take a look at it. Yes, in his job there would be often false alarms, but on Boxing Day evening in the completely different world of 1964, did the officer truly have anything else to do? Mum and Alan were without choice. They returned home, briefly filling a small void in time that would become an enormous one in all of our lives.

Our neighbour, Margaret, was left at home with us kids. We all waited every long second for Mum to burst through the door with Lesley. And when only Mum and Alan emerged, it was obvious in seconds that the worst was still to come. No screams of joy, no relief, no words at all. In short, no Lesley. The atmosphere spoke the words.

Even Brett realised that something was going on. All of us sensed that doing nothing contributed to the crime. Alan got that more than anyone. Mum had barely taken her coat off when their nervous energy – or determined focus – told them that the children would wait and that being in the house was futile.

That meant racking the brain for places Lesley might have been. We have all in life retraced our steps and second-guessed where we could have misplaced something trivial. You explore likely scenarios and hopeful places. You clutch at straws until one of them comes good for you. When you reflect, most of what you seek is replaceable. This was totally different in that we were looking everywhere for something – *someone* – for which there was no substitute. The only parallel is that we were clutching ... at straws.

Alan suggested heading for the derelict mill. Mum didn't even know where he meant. The North West was littered with them. He meant Butler Street and the old cotton mill. There was no way Lesley would have gone there. We all knew that. But there was also no way Lesley would have not come home. Every suggestion, however much a wildcard felt like they were doing something. Idle, like the policeman, was betrayal. For your own nervous energy in the moment, and I suppose in the years after, you wanted to look yourself in the mirror and say that you did everything you could. The inactions of the police station single-handedly triggered that rear-guard action.

But just like the stream before, they got no response, other than the echo of their own voices, and they returned home to all of us sobbing. My brothers were taken up to bed, but I was now wide awake, immune to illness, and telling Mum that nobody would hurt our Les.

I don't know what I truly believed. I am not sure if I really understood what hurt meant. I cannot comprehend why I was trying to re-assure Mum. My own guilt just kept me talking. I knew something was horribly wrong and I was responsible.

Mum pacified me – a sort of reflex reaction for her and for me. People were beginning to say the right things, believing that was beneficial too. I was disbelieving and knew nothing was helping. I know she was caught in the crossfire of having to deal with three confused children, when the reality was that Lesley's fate, at the most magical time of year, had imposed tragedy on us for an eternity.

Mum made provisions for the next day, asking Margaret if she might be on standby. That did not sound re-assuring to anybody, however young you were. Then she remembered that Auntie Elsie and Uncle John had not turned up and this gave her hope too, believing that Lesley might have gone there on the bus.

Off they went again, in search of public transport to make the seven-mile trip to our relatives, who could only apologise for their no-show at ours. And no, they didn't have Lesley. They were stunned to see Mum and Alan show up. The level of concern was now such that Elsie and John came back to ours, and with them, came the sort of optimistic hope that we had all clung to like Alan and the mill, in that they brought new ideas, and with that fresh promise and renewed energy. A new person, a new location, a new thought – it felt like you were doing something.

They killed time – 'chain-smoking' coffee. There was almost none left by the time Alan rose to announce that they were going back to the police station. I don't know what time it was because there was no sense of it any more – the remnants of Christmas stood frozen and silent like statues, with food untouched, television unwatched and presents, so lovingly cherished 24 hours earlier, now abandoned. The stillness of the festive materialism ran headlong into the agitation in the dialogue. It added to the notion that we were culpable by doing nothing. The world had stopped in every sense and Alan wanted to counter that.

Outside, the joy of revellers exiting pubs broke the Christmas trance. Even at my age then, drunkenness had never seemed so pointless as that night. We were the only people in a hurry who had nothing to laugh about.

At the station, Mum and Alan's re-appearance brought the desk sergeant back to life. I suspect he didn't think he would see them again, but a second showing within the time frame he had outlined meant that this was now escalating. Nobody can ever be certain if this delay was significant. Police will often cite that first 60 minutes as being key in a missing persons case. You like to think it might have made a difference but you can't know that. You run that line through your head to have someone to blame. I only felt that I had myself to blame, though.

Finally, now, Mum and Alan were given an audience, but it was already too much. The delay and the initial visit to the station were tearing her apart and going through the rigmarole of the basics about Lesley's appearance, movements and friends delayed a search further, whilst obviously vital to any such operation. From those details, one of the biggest manhunts in British criminal history began. It went from almost dismissive to full-on overdrive, and when Mum walked back into the house, clearly still without my sister, I was once again waiting for her on the couch, distraught. Only on her say so did I go to bed and then just lay there long into the night, against a backdrop of raised voices and sobbing, doors opening occasionally, offering false hope, and Mum climbing the stairs to my sister's room to leave a light on and open the curtains. Symbolic gestures, I now understand were open signs of grief and false strength, when to others, they looked like you were just going through the motions.

In the silences from downstairs, when nobody knew what to say, the void where you imagine you have heard Lesley coming home as your mind plays tricks deafens you as you try to sleep.

It was too late. She was never coming back.

Chapter 4

It is now 27 December. I only know that because it is the first day after Boxing Day. Stress and fatigue equal exhaustion. I know I slept a little because naturally you awake with almost Christmas Day nerves to sneak downstairs to see if Lesley is home. It is the same sensation of expectation and the unknown, but at different ends of the anxiety scale.

Mum was in a state. Worse than I remember when I went to bed. She looked like she hadn't gone up at all. It was clear too from the smell that the world would soon run out of tobacco. A minor kerfuffle of hope had woken me – any noise offered that.

There was only despair.

'Why hasn't Les come home?' she sobbed and screamed.

'What has happened to Lesley?'

These were the only two questions from now on and we didn't stop repeating them as though we had never uttered these words before. A new person would walk in and this same short despairing conversation would begin again. I was up before Brett and Tommy so I got it first. They were only the questions that I was asking too.

It was never a dialogue. I would say the same even if I was just repeating what Mum said.

'Where has she gone?' I asked, knowing that evil had been bestowed upon her but probably too young to fully grasp the concept of kidnap, abduction and murder.

'We don't know, she's not come home,' Mum answered staring into space.

And that told you one thing – that the second visit to the police station had brought nothing so far.

By the time I went downstairs, Mum and Alan had already been down to the paper shop on Bradford Road. They were almost lone figures in the street as they had been the previous evening, but in the queue, there were plenty all asking

24

the same question – had people heard about the little girl who had gone missing from the fairground the previous night?

And there it was – the headlines were confirming it. Lesley was front page news. Somehow while we were giving details and being questioned ourselves, the 'story' gathered legs and the grapevine began. Never in a million years would anyone in our family be newsworthy. Now, the process began which would never leave us. On that particular day in 1964, I could have no idea that I would still have the media in my life in 2017 and how that media would then be. For Mum, it was the beginning of a love-hate relationship, which she understood the need for awareness of Lesley's disappearance, but over time would prove to be testing and unpredictable too.

At home, they read the articles. I saw it on the TV news too. They were just words and it was just noise. I could not really understand that the box in the corner that had been a world of magic and mystery was now bringing us the news that my sister was missing. They were talking and writing about my Lesley, but she was ours and not theirs. She belonged in this room and not on the news. They spoke of her as if they knew her. The only hope that Mum took was learning from the media that all police leave had now been recalled – a massive contrast from the indifference of the first time they called at the station. We began to detest having the TV on at all. Firstly, our lives were public. Secondly, there was nothing new. So, hope was fading. It condemned us further, haunting us like Lesley's room.

Alan was holding it together. He had to. Nobody else had any sense of rationale – mood swings were constant and the persistent knocking at the door from well-wishers, police, nosey-parkers and close friends and family meant that the only consistency to the atmosphere was its inconsistency. Every new arrival meant those same two questions again and the process re-started. The continual flow through the front door meant it appeared as though it was support and kind-hearted people willing to help, but of course, it added to the nervous tension and stress which were the seeds of what then became a lifetime of anxiety for my Mum.

In between the arrivals, Mum would sit down and sometimes go back up to Lesley's room. What was meant as a positive message of hope in leaving Lesley's bedroom ready for her return was fast becoming a shrine. The open curtains and made-up bed that were to welcome her back began to underline the point more that she hadn't been home at all. The room started to stare back at us. Lesley's sewing machine, which was a gift from our real Dad, just sat there downstairs. In her excitement, she had used it just once, believing there were plenty more happy weekends and holidays to wile away the time on it. It was never used again.

I was feeling stronger physically, but had never felt worse, mentally. I understand today this was the beginning of delayed shock. I was drawn to returning to the fair.

There was little point. Lesley was not ever going to be there and I couldn't retrace *our* steps as I hadn't gone with her the previous night. It was a desperate lonely miserable exercise. Placing yourself at the scene might help deal with it. It didn't. It made it worse. Years later, when I was a delivery driver, I had to go past the parkland area every single day. Every time I did it, I returned to Boxing Day 1964.

At home, Tommy and Brett remained clueless to the details of what was going on, but the atmosphere of sobbing and screaming hid them from nothing else. My youngest brother still played with his toys – the only semblance of normality in a home where normal would never come again. I know Tommy too felt that silent guilt. He just assumed Les had gone ahead of him.

Word was clearly spreading. Somehow my real Dad had known straightaway and we didn't have a phone to call him. But still, there were no sightings, no clothing and no timings. As I reflect years later with a greater understanding of the world and with much more experience of watching crime being reported, the fact that nobody could say they had seen Lesley *and* without any certainty of a timeline, was staggering.

26

This was Boxing Day and a busy place where everybody went each and every year. To this day, it has bugged me. How many times do you think I have asked 'Surely, somebody must have seen something?' But there was nothing. In a more innocent time, hiding in broad daylight looks to have been very easy to do.

Mum was losing it increasingly, convinced that Lesley was still alive – or at least she told us that was her belief. At fourteen, it was hard to contemplate death. 'Not home' was sufficiently distressing because of the worry. Death, at least, was finite. Despite saying this, I remember Mum changing clothes on that first afternoon. She came downstairs in black as though already acknowledging the worst.

Alan could see her slipping away – us three boys just existed. We were almost parentless. Late in the afternoon, that became a reality with a hefty knock on the door.

Chapter 5

Alan answered the thud and ushered two CID officers in. I was trying to listen from behind the door. This had to mean something. It must be some sort of news. But there was still no Lesley and no child running to greet Mum. The tone of the voices, the pauses between the words, the lack of frenetic energy made it clear.

There *was* no good news. In fact, the opposite was true. I heard one of the officers asking Mum and Alan to come to the station.

Might there be news there? Could there be something to identify or did they need more information? I would have to wait. Mum and Alan were off again, leaving one of my best friend's Mums, Margaret to babysit. I watched them go in the police car, sobbing my eyes out once more. I knew it was serious if they were leaving. So many people had come to the house, including the police, that for them to leave not of their own accord meant the worst.

We had tried to keep occupied all day, without really doing anything, except sitting tight and wanting a development. Now something was happening, it created a new stress. They had definitely not delivered any bad news in the house. I had to satisfy myself that the police would not draw out a car journey to the station and make them wait further if they had something definitive to say. I just had to be patient and see, and wondering what was happening was crucifying.

They had both been taken into individual interview rooms and asked by a detective and policewoman much of what they had already told them the previous night. Then came a tone which my Mum never forgot.

Had they beaten or molested the children?

They tried to play Mum against Alan, stereotyping stepfathers, when we saw him more than our real Dad and were clearly settled now in the calmest period of our lives. In short, we saw Alan as Dad. Stepfather was a word only the police were using.

Had Mum ever smacked us? Had Lesley ever been forward with Alan? Mum was already in a bad enough state and, of course, it would never have occurred to her that she and Alan could become suspects. She was torn apart with the early stages of grief and now that turned to rage – so much so that the female officer had to restrain her. And it went on for hours, with interrogations on Lesley's history of running away, of which there was none…or if the stress of Christmas had been to blame. There had been no stress. We were settled.

And of course, neither Mum nor Alan knew what the other was being asked and both were united in their denial. It was only their manner that differed with Mum hysterical and Alan much colder and calmer.

When the officers decided to suspend questioning for the night, Mum walked back into the waiting area of the police station, her grief, anger and stress exploded. There was my brother, Tommy, in his pyjamas and duffel coat at the age of eight at 10 pm balling his eyes. I remember the knock at the door when they came for him too. The previous day had been upsetting enough. There was no need for it to be this late. But they took him away, despite the fact that he was asleep, bundling him into a police car and submitting him to an hour's worth of questioning about Lesley, Mum and of course, the mystery of the wicked stepfather. You read now of heavy-handed police tactics, but this was 1964.

I didn't really understand like I do today, except to be aware that you couldn't rule anything out. The police never came to the house to question me. They *did* need to speak Tommy – of course. He had probably been one of the last to see her at the fair, but this was not their tone or line of inquiry. If they really wanted to persist with that innuendo then that could come later. Nobody, to this point had asked my brother to tell them what he could remember from just 24 hours before.

When the three of them returned together, I was waiting petrified to know why Tommy had gone too. I didn't really understand about giving eye-witness statements, so I certainly could not comprehend what Mum explained to me had happened, especially as her and Alan were still getting to grips with comparing each other's accounts. My relief at seeing all three come home subsided in seconds when obviously there was still no Lesley and there was still no news. Everybody felt we had gone backwards. Then I saw the two officers with the three of them. They were coming into the house, making Alan take them through every room, even though Brett was asleep. Mum looked awful. Tommy was exhausted. Alan just took them round, flat-batting blatant accusations that he knew where Lesley was, even having to open the airing cupboard to show that she was not hiding there. I could hear all the commotion upstairs sat by the fire, still crying my eyes out. The low point was when they searched the bins.

Finally, they left after what must have been an hour or so. I know it was a crushing blow for both to deal with, especially Alan, when all they were doing was trying to find Lesley. One type of grief and despair became another, a different one as they became the suspects. For Mum, it was more and more time frittering away, besides from being a ridiculous allegation. The happiest little girl in the world had opened her sewing machine and skipped off to the fair. Of *course*, she would then choose Boxing Evening to run away because she was being beaten at home. Obviously.

Chapter 6

Boxing Day had rolled into the 27th and that in turn into the 28th. There was no let up. It was the same scenario every day, except for two differences. There was no more suggestive tone from the police, and the arrivals at the house from people whom we knew began to subside. The visits to the station and back to ours continued, but the slur had disappeared and neighbours did still call in, but didn't stay for as long. Their own lives were getting back to normal.

As less and less friends and family turned up, more and more unknowns replaced them – from nosey busy-bodies to a baiting press. This was now life as we knew it.

After the festivities, people had one eye on New Year and then the return to reality. Ours had changed forever. The spirit of Christmas was diminishing, whilst the tree and decorations stayed up, increasingly out of place, amidst our fear and grief, yet remaining like monuments, like Lesley's room – untouched, as though we were freezing the moment in time in the hope that we could reset that clock at a moment's notice.

There was *always* hope until told otherwise, but after the first night it fell away rapidly, and now the familiar disappointment and renewed heartache began afresh every morning when I climbed down the stairs to see Mum through a haze of tobacco, still crying and screaming, shouting unanswerable questions into the air, while Alan pacified. I knew of course now by the time I went down every morning that Les wasn't there. The whole house would have erupted with joy whatever the time of day if there had been news. But still there was nothing. Not a flicker. No sightings, no clothing and no timings.

And so, it continued. The year's end did not bring the curtain down on anything at all for us. I barely noticed as 1964 became 1965. Should old acquaintances be forgot and never brought to mind? I didn't really understand what it meant, but I knew the answer.

How on earth could we carry on? We weren't even trudging through life. There was no new hope on the horizon with the turning of the calendar. We just stared and cried. The scene was frozen at Boxing Day 1964 and somehow, we had to find a way. Life had to go on, but when? Those decorations stayed up as winter really set in and Lesley's room, you would probably conclude, was indeed a shrine. In the first 24 hours when it tries to radiate that positivity that your room is ready for you when you come home, its untouched state just resonates 'never coming home'.

Mum somehow had to get us ready for school. By that point, I knew and we all knew that somebody had got Les and she wasn't coming back, even though education back then never included 'stranger danger' and warnings about engaging with people you didn't know. Safety warnings were more likely to be about level crossings and playing at the disused mill. I didn't even know the word abduction. I am not really aware of what was said, but I know Mum spoke with the Head, Mr Williams who, of course, already knew. Everybody did. Both were concerned that the press might be sniffing around and that obviously had implications for me, but also the whole school in a less media-aware time. There was not much news over Christmas and we were it. I wore that glazed look into the playground. I didn't speak a lot and nobody bullied me about Lesley. Kids can be cruel sometimes without knowing the extent of their venom, but I was spared and term time became the distraction I needed. At least the hours between nine and three got me out of the house, and whilst that emptiness and hollowness inside was shared amongst the family, it was not a healthy environment. Mum was going downhill fast, now on a regular supply of about ten sedatives a day, and often booze.

The only respite was the church. Mum's relationship with the Lord was now highly questionable, but we still attended every week for the sense of community that it brought, and if there really was a God then she could place that hope at his altar. For a while, that provides strength. Over time, it erodes that belief and it rebounds on itself. A credence you placed such trust in falls apart at the seams when there is no promised land. When the one thing you pray for does not turn up, you either pray some more or stop for good. We experienced both. At least in that environment when you were there, calmness and peace prevailed and you were surrounded by good people who cared. The neighbourhood clubbed together in January to raise £100. They didn't have much, especially after Christmas, and didn't need to show such kindness, but the gravity of the situation had clearly resonated because this money was for posters to display Lesley's face all over Manchester. A month had nearly passed and it must have taken a week or so to organise, but our community obviously woke up post New Year to the sense that something had to be done when it looked like nothing was. It gave belief and anguish. It might trigger a sighting. There was still time. Hope was renewed. Yet her image was staring back at us and that haunted too.

Her picture radiated innocence. Lesley's name was in capitals and in full as Lesley Ann *Downey.*

'*Missing from her home in Ancoats, Manchester, since 4.30 pm 26th December 1964. Ten years, 4.10, Slim Build, Blue Eyes, Brown Hair, Fair Complexion. Wearing Tartan Dress, Blue Coat, Pink Cardigan, Red Shoes. Any Information Telephone Chief Constable Manchester City Police.*'

Looking back at it now, I realise there is a glaring omission. It said nothing about the fair. It wouldn't have made a difference in finding Lesley, but we might have got to the information quicker and saved other victims. She did not go missing from her home. That was simply wrong and a massive mistake. But at the time, we were clearly not experts in this kind of thing and heavily reliant on our generous, kind neighbours.

That spirit was borne out of the church. It also became Lesley's second shrine. She was always radiant on a Sunday and there wasn't a week when we stood there when we couldn't see her. To attend, therefore meant a proximity to her. You could sense Les in the room, whereas at home her spirit had flown.

Our neighbour, Mrs Clark had also left. I didn't notice at the time, but Mum told me later and, as the years passed, I have only drawn the conclusion that the stress of living so close to us and feeling slightly the responsibility for Lesley on that night drove her away. The unwanted attention at our door and the row that Mum and her had that evening must have left her no choice. I don't know what became of her and like me, if she had gone to the fair then Lesley would have been alive. I say that with no malice, more an acknowledgement of the secondary grief that she and her little girl must have felt until the day she died.

But *we* also had asked the council to move on in the May. I decided to stay briefly behind to finish the school year. I don't know if I wanted distance from home or if I had found in education a family life that home was now cruelly not allowed to provide. It certainly wasn't because I was academic. For Mum, the constant barrage from the press and fanatics probably persuaded her that, whilst there should be no escape and you couldn't start again, the only way to begin to repair was to move. You couldn't stay in that house. So, as she had done many times before, she found the strength to take herself off to the Housing Office and demanded a move, without needing to resort to the tricks that took us fatefully to Charnley Walk.

With the move to Holy Trinity we knew that we were taking a risk in that it was now too far to sustain our church commitments and had to inform Reverend Ford that, despite his compassion, always making way for us and inviting Mum to pick hymns, that we would no longer be part of his congregation. This meant potentially a huge void in our lives. Despite our questionable stance now on whether the Lord really was looking down on us, that regularity of Sundays and that calmness that it brought was to disappear. We would have to find a new church closer to home.

The generosity of the funds raised for the poster campaign was now dwarfed by what happened next. Knowing he had probably seen us for the last time, we were all invited to the vicarage for Sunday lunch only to learn that it was a ruse. In the street stood a car – a parting gift meant to enable us to still attend, but also go wherever the search for Lesley might take us.

I was ecstatic, despite the circumstances. Having a car was something we could never have dreamt of. Alan had use of a van in the past for work, but affording a real family car was never going to be possible. We were speechless and embarrassed. It was an incredible gesture, but too much and we had to decline, only to be told that it was not an option.

The kindness of the community shone forth once more.

The seasons changed, the school year rolled on to its conclusion and birthdays came and went. The abnormality of numbness was the norm. I do not even remember 21 August 1965. It would have been Lesley's 11th birthday. The day is blacked out. I am sure the small number of people who have found themselves in the midst of tragedy like this will tell you that the first year of passing those anniversaries is so very painful – not just the major ones, like your date of birth or the next Boxing Day, but all those that Lesley would have been part of too, like her best friends or her brothers, and then there are those days that are just moments which every parent has from the first day of the school year and going up a class, to Easters and summer holidays. Somebody was always missing and it was Lesley, and in that first twelve months it hurt so bad. By August, we had acceptance. Lesley was only part of our lives in our memories. She could have actually been alive, Mum always maintained, held against her will by some evil perpetrator, but she was no longer ours, wherever she was. Mum never gave up, but also reached some sort of acceptance. And so, on Lesley's birthday, there was no symbolic card or cake. What on earth do you do on a day like that? Do you make a new shrine and 'go through the motions', showing the ultimate in sensitivity by still wrapping presents so she remains alive in your mind and so you can show her when she comes home that you remembered her every day and on her special day, or do you block it out because that is the very real truth? There is no Lesley, so there is no birthday. I remember only the subdued atmosphere. We carried on. We got through. And then we carried on some more.

The interest of the press never subsided. I accept now that it was a massive story and we were grateful at times when it looked like people had forgotten, but that also meant journalists snooping when there was nothing new to add, and the downside of the re-reporting and looking for new angles which didn't exist meant that I watched Mum dealing with abuse and cranks too. Only with time and exposure to other tragedies and crimes do I understand that events like these attract 'fans' and a group of individuals who measure their own lot in parallel. Most were anonymous and Mum was now so immune to emotion beyond that which she felt for Lesley that the sheer volume of abuse didn't increase any strain on her. The reverse was true. It gave her resolve to brush it off. The compassionate were a wonderful source of comfort, but those who chose to attack Mum were met with short change at the house. One or two letters might have derailed her further, but plenty actually made it easier.

The family kept many of them for years – often the tone was that Mum should be grateful because she still had the rest of us left. At my age, I thought it was horrific and of course, I didn't understand journalism or stalking. All I really could comprehend was that the presence of both was chipping away at the whole family. Going to school or church and every day there was somebody unrecognisable beyond their identification by trade or weirdness. It meant that I finally snapped, leaving a note pinned to the front door, asking anybody with any information regarding my sister's disappearance to tell the family. I could have done this on Boxing Day, but it was the constant scrutiny that made me do so only many months after. The presence of so many people interested in our lives served me personally with one reminder.

It underlined my guilt.

Chapter 7

Many of these people who came into our world you might call crackpots. Some, even as late as 2017, followed that pattern of people who were drawn to our lives for all sorts of motives, though a few claimed to have escaped Lesley's captors. In 2017, we are aware of conspiracy theories and that social media can now give the village idiot a voice, but then you also took people at face value.

It is clear to me, looking back, that in fact, people weren't all good. They just did not have the audience that they do now. In the beginning, it was so difficult to know where the line was from people whom you knew knocking at your door to the lady on Bradford Road who organised the collection for the posters. These were good people, but in amongst them merged some individuals whom we took as sincere, but clearly were not.

If there was a point when our guard went up, it must have begun with the night the police turned the tables on us. I was fourteen – brought up to believe that they were a pillar of the community, who walked the streets and nodded at you and, that if being late home once incurred a rollicking from Mum, then you certainly did not want to incur their wrath. I had never had experience with the police before, beyond a hello and they weren't all they seemed to be. Today, I understand that in many missing persons cases they *do* look to people the child knows – often in the family. But this was *my* family they were talking about and I knew it was rubbish and with their actions, it set down a marker of suspicion that flowed over into my view of society at large.

Now, of course, the police did attempt to make amends, justifying that it was a moment they had to get past and I do accept that now, but at fourteen it was akin to breaking a code with a child, like Santa not existing. Here was my first experience with the upholders of the law and suddenly we were criminals and I was potentially a witness against my own parents.

I didn't have the words to express what I felt at the time and the years do give me that clarity, but inside in 1964, I know I was muted with fear that was spiralling out of control and that manifested itself in the note I left and in relations with the press, my decision to stay on when the family moved, and all of our guards going up when new people arrived on the horizon.

Many *did* mean well, but everybody unknown to us who came into our lives played with our emotions, whether intentionally or not. For Mum, it just meant more medication.

If you genuinely knew something then why leave it beyond the first 48 hours? Why were you only just showing up the following summer? There could only be two reasons – guilt at what you knew or morbid fascination. And the only guilt we seemed to have experienced from other people was Mrs Clark who had left. There had been a reward of course and the power of that cannot be underestimated. So wary and weary, we still found ourselves in a difficult situation because any one of these individuals still knocking down our door or writing to us might have a tiny nugget of something or could just be glory hunters. There were genuinely a huge number of people who did tell us they knew something only to raise our hopes and dash them again. I think now I understand that if you do have information and are a stranger, you go to the police first and not the family. If you want parallels, look at the false leads the McCanns have had over the years – and people can make a little name for themselves with all the media and social media today. But it was happening then too. Sick games from people who had nothing better to do than cause us further grief, citing Lesley on a bus here or even with a family in Belgium. Whilst living with no news was exhausting and excruciating, fantasists whom you had to entertain to explore every possibility wore you down even more and eroded that soul which saw the good in Reverend Ford and a collecting congregation, but also now looked at the police with eyes in the back of your head.

Just to prove the point that Mum in particular did entertain these people to a point, she somehow was put in contact with a clairvoyant from Holland called Emile Croiset. I didn't know what the word meant and I probably couldn't find you The Netherlands on a map back then. To date I can't picture this person because there were just so many who came to the house. I only remember the story and the fact that Mum gave more credence than anyone to this individual, because we were assured that he had a pretty decent record in helping the police with missing persons.

The whole concept of 'missing persons' was relatively new to us – it began on Boxing Day. But here was someone whom the police trusted and had been doing this for sometime. It made you realise that Lesley was not the isolated case that we had told ourselves she was. We hadn't really considered that she might be one of many. Without realising it, to have this man in our presence for around a month on and off, sewed the seed that perhaps it was not just Lesley.

For now, we just wanted Les back and with so much emotional energy spent on both well-intended and malice-laden false hope, we gave Emile as much opportunity as anyone else.

It depends on your viewpoint in life, but you would be forgiven for thinking this would all end in tears too. We had been here once before when a lady who claimed to have special powers, but was no more than a drunken old fool, persuaded Mum and Alan that Lesley was buried in Deansgate, Manchester and so desperate for answers were they that they began digging on their knees with their bare hands in the city centre. This presented the conundrum. 'Disappointment' at not finding Lesley still gave birth to false hope. Devastated to be taken in and find nothing, it meant that Lesley must still be alive. In short, that personified the problem. It was highly unlikely that Lesley was in Deansgate – of her own accord or at the hands of someone else. She wouldn't go there and why would an abductor be so indiscreet close to the centre of the second biggest city in the country? And now a second clairvoyant? From Holland? In Manchester? You can see we were truly out of options. And more to the point, so were the police.

From what Mum told me, he approached his work studiously. It is just a question of whether you can get past the clairvoyance. Our relationship with the church was fragile, despite the kindness and the gifts. When it came to it, the Lord had not delivered Lesley. This was similar spiritual territory, except that we believed God would surely come good because we held faith in him, though that led to disappointment. With Emile, there was no expectation.

I remember Mum and Alan coming back from the police station where he had sat them down. It was not good.

He told them that he could see the body of a child in a field. There had been a struggle. She had fought for her life, but she did not die there. There were four people and they were near water. One had a motorbike.

I sat there open-mouthed. It was more detail than anybody had provided and my parents hadn't hidden anything from us. There were genuinely no leads. This was the first expression of confidence. This was the first sighting – even if it was in his mind. Mum said he didn't waiver. He spoke it as he saw it and with conviction. He was not the fantasist that others had been.

With the police and my parents, they had left the station to visit the site of the fair, now obviously unrecognisable from Boxing Day. Apart from the pictures in his head Emile could have no clarity of what that scene looked like before, whereas we had seen it year after year. I don't know if he therefore had fresh perspective.

But he highlighted a road that divided at a fork, outlined a cemetery and said that people had taken Lesley and they had gone on the low road.

That was the end of the line. He couldn't see and didn't know beyond that, but it was more than anyone had offered.

The information, if true, was probably too late to use and would anyone have actually seen them there on Boxing Day night?

There was no evidence. It was just one man's vision. And it remained the only *fragile* concrete hope to cling to, but led us nowhere. In the moment, it could be passed off as a speculative hunch. Over the years, it has battered my head that somebody could see what nobody else could, because what we were to discover in time, was that either Emile had either got very lucky or he had got it very right.

Chapter 8

I left school with nothing – no qualifications and less ambition. Like many, I just wanted to start my life properly. Regrettably, I couldn't start it again, but I had a chance to break free from the shackles of education and, even though I moved back in with Mum, Alan and the boys when the academic year was done, I think both the end of school and the new property were at least an attempt to move on. I began working an apprenticeship at Walter Ashworth's – the butcher in Hyde.

I simply walked into town and asked who needed work and found myself learning the trade six days a week for a pittance for the best part of a year. I enjoyed it. The discipline was different to being at school and having my own money in my pocket was, like anybody at that age, an absolute dream. Mum still had her house rules, of course, even though she was slipping away with the drugs, but I was now treated a little differently and seeing life from a brand-new viewpoint.

I won't say I was happy, but for the first time since Boxing Day, I had some sense of purpose. But of course, just when you think you are moving into a slightly better place, a thunderbolt out of the blue knocks you for six.

Saturday night TV. We are watching as a family when they suddenly cut into the show to announce that the body of a child had been found in a shallow grave on Saddleworth Moor, near Manchester. I didn't know where that was. The report did not have any more information, other than that they were going to make an identification soon. It was rare for a TV show to be interrupted, unless it was of national importance. I didn't realise the significance of the bulletin, but it sent Mum into overdrive, screaming 'Not my Lesley – please God', which I thought at the time was very strange, because nobody from the police had contacted us or asked us to go to the station again.

It couldn't be Lesley and who would do such a thing? But Mum *knew* then and was shaking uncontrollably, worse than ever. She had to get to the phone at a neighbour's house and struggled to dial the police.

'Is the body on the moor Lesley? Is Lesley dead?' she sobbed.

But the officer said not.

Mum wasn't having it, urging him to put her out of her misery and not taking no for an answer.

'It is the body of a boy,' he told her, to which she accused him of lying.

He calmly spoke the same words again and urged Mum to go back home.

'Thank God,' she cried into Alan's chest. 'It's not Lesley. Thank God.'

It is now Sunday 17 October, 1965.

Alan was wide awake that morning, staring out of the window; Mum had been temporarily lost to medicine. She came around slowly, as she did most days, and Alan couldn't bring himself to utter the words.

'It's the press,' I heard him say. 'They are everywhere. The street is full of them.'

I could see for myself too.

You didn't need anyone to add words to the pictures. It was clear what was going on.

The media had been a constant in the last ten months. Some days were busier than others. Most days there would always be somebody. Today, you couldn't move for reporters and photographers and it was a Sunday. What should have been a quiet day had turned into a feeding frenzy. How did they all know something that we did not? Neighbours' curtains were twitching too. We had seen that before, but this was different.

I felt anxiety rise through my ribs. I was looking for some sort of guidance from my parents. Alan's tone was different. The upbeat voice keeping Mum going for so many months had been reduced to few words. I watched her rise towards the window and look out on a sea of TV trucks and cars parked just wherever they could. I could see she was struggling. I know I had that sickly feeling in my stomach, taking my lead from outside, which despite all we had previously endured, was on another level, dwarfing previous media contingents. But I read Mum and Alan instinctively as she sunk to her knees, collapsing in a heap. We had been through much negativity – days and nights of wailing and sobbing and others too of silence. But this was different.

Mum knew. Alan knew. I knew.

'It's our Lesley,' she attempted to whisper, while Alan laid her down on the bed and urged her that actually we had not been told a thing at this point. But for the first time in ten months, the rock had been chipped away. Even I could hear that he didn't sound like he meant it. We had experienced so many people who remained positive for us and had tried to say the right thing, but now Alan knew the game was up.

Then there were two loud knocks at the door.

We were barely dressed and clearly hours behind everyone else. I followed Mum and Alan towards the entrance of the house as they grabbed dressing gowns and coats to keep warm. I don't know if it was a cold October morning or if the house was damp. We were all just shaking, shivering with fear.

And then the moment we had been dreading. Breathless with angst, I watched Alan unbolt the lock to see two plain-clothes policemen standing there. I caught sight of them briefly before the flashbulbs forced us to recoil, dazzled in the headlights. Outside, the murmur and hubbub was rising to fever pitch. The officers' tone was calm and apologetic, but their demeanour was uncomfortable.

Next came words that have replayed in our heads over and over again since.

'Mrs Downey, it is our sad duty to ask you to come to the mortuary to make a formal identification.'

Nobody spoke. The officers looked at the floor then began to weep themselves. Mum was gone. In a daze of denial – the room spinning and her soul shaking with pain. Alan tried to stabilise her. I was white and again reduced to mute.

Mum began to plead.

'You said it was a little boy,' she begged, referring to last night's call.

'It might not be Lesley,' one of the officers offered unconvincingly. 'We just can't be sure.'

I sat on the stairs watching, frozen with panic, but alert enough to know that this just did not tally with anything that Mum had heard on the phone. That was twice now the police had let us down.

But it was the second officer who showed that they were being economical with the truth. I understand now that it is a thankless task, but language is a giveaway.

'We need you to come and look at the clothes the little girl was wearing,' he blundered.

As far as we could all make out, people generally were not going missing and there was certainly only one little girl in this area that merited this attention and scrutiny.

It was a crushing blow. How could they have been so convinced last night that it was definitely a boy and there was nothing to worry about? I could see too the discomfort in both of them – the silence condemned them and us as everyone realised that one of the pair had inadvertently dropped an almighty clanger. I knew for sure. My parents did too and they, without question were certain.

I realise there are procedures and, until a body is identified, nothing is concluded, but given the context, we were effectively condemned. The last ten months had been hell. That Boxing Day cursed Christmas forever. Living without Lesley for both her beautiful presence while she was here and my own guilt at what happened had been soul destroying. I personally had tried to move on a little.

Only now was the nightmare truly beginning.

Chapter 9

What followed is what Mum told me just once. She rarely ever spoke of it again.

As ever the police were ahead of her and Alan. It was becoming a scenario where the police now knew the answers to the questions they were about to answer. And yet, I felt such anguish and anger at the call last night. We had waited months for news and then found out via the television. Our hopes were raised – but they weren't, were they? We didn't want news that Lesley was dead. These are now the parameters. People say no news is good news. We wanted news. We saw the news. Our hopes were raised. But what were those hopes when there was a report of a grave? We got swept along and Mum made the call and was told otherwise. So, we are relieved but deflated because the news is not ours, yet that could only have been bad news. It is an unfathomable web of expectation and emotion.

So, we go to bed, 'hopes' raised and dashed but with then renewed 'hope'. It is the first news that we have heard since the clairvoyant, but there is no news. Therefore, we are safe but ultimately back where we were and with no advancement. A false alarm that was ultimately pointless, except to wake us. It is an impossible situation that you hope for information and you think it may be finally here and then it isn't. Are you relieved that there is still no 'closure' or would you have been relieved that there finally was? This is the mental impact.

Then you wake the next morning and you know that you *are* grateful there is nothing to report. You have clarity and your thoughts turn to whoever the brothers and sisters and parents of the little boy might be and you assume 'thank God, it is not us' mentality. You have escaped. You have no new news, but you live to fight another day and the false alarm creates new hope and increased vigour. We must do posters again and put the word out there once more.

But the thunderous knock at the door came before we really had a chance to process all of this and, before I knew it, Mum and Alan were off against the glare of the flashbulbs, heading once more to the police station. What if it wasn't Lesley? What if they were on the way to identify someone else's child? That would be distressing enough, apart from the fact that we knew it wasn't true.

Mum took an age to get dressed and find someone to look after us. She didn't want to leave, but had to. This was the day she had been waiting on for over the last ten months, but hoped would never come. She was going so very slowly and now was not the time to be babysat. The boys maybe – but I needed to go too. It was my fault. I ran towards Mum on her way out and locked myself within her. I can see it today. It tells you that I knew and I was devastated for me, but also had some sort of sense of what Mum was about to endure – let alone what we were yet to discover. I had no idea of what the next procedure was. I was still too young. I was almost regressing from a young adult back to a child younger than Our Les. But sometimes when you don't know the detail, you understand the drama.

But then I did what I had done before. I am the little boy sobbing into Mum's chest but trying to find words to re-assure her. All I could find were those I had uttered before.

'Nobody would hurt our Les,' I said.

And I genuinely believed it, even though it was now becoming obvious that somebody had.

'Its not going to be our Lesley,' I wailed. And then broke down on the floor.

I was a child and a young adult – trying to becalm Mum with comforting words, but also seeking maternal love, offering confidence in my words, but like the policeman, no longer believing them. Maturity. Immaturity. Being the parent and needing the parent. Trying to tell Mum it was all OK, when it was my fault that it was not. Offering re-assurance. Needing re-assurance.

Mum did not want to leave me. I did not want to leave Mum. She kissed me and made for the door, guided by Alan and the policemen. I cried even more and screamed as she left. She passed me like a ghost drifting through walls.

The only respite was the unwelcome one. Mum's daze and my helplessness led to an open door. The police led the way. There could not have been a worse moment. Microphones, cameras, flashbulbs. Lights, cameras, action.

And we froze. The baying mob stood within metres. They knew the fate that we did not. We were public property all over again. Even the cops struggled to fend off the journalists, each of them thrusting their equipment our way without a scent of compassion, all desperate for the story.

It was a pointless exercise. We had nothing to say. What on earth were they trying to achieve? If they were that ahead of the game that they knew to come to the house when we had been told nothing, then surely, they would be smart enough to go to the police station or Saddleworth itself? It was obvious that Mum would have nothing to say, but then if they wanted a picture of a woman who looked like she had seen a ghost then they had it. Mum's existence now was only physical. The spirit had left her.

I could see Mum almost thrown into the back seat of the police car, flanked by Alan and an officer. The media followed relentlessly. They wanted the shots, but they would learn little. We knew nothing.

They left at high speed, tearing at an urgency that would look timid in today's world, but I knew then rang alarm bells. It was part avoidance of the press, part urgency to get to the mortuary. That is how the moment catches up with you. Dead is dead. It doesn't matter how quickly you go, because you can't change anything, but adrenaline, even for the cops experienced at driving fast, incentivised the race to get there. If it were Lesley – or indeed anyone – then you had all day and all night to turn up. There was no bringing her back. But when *you* are in that situation, haste appears to be part of the non-existent solution.

Mum told me they were pursued all the way, tyres burning. When they arrived, the officers, who had attempted to be tranquil before, were rushing them in as Alan tried to shield Mum's face with a blanket, and the press who *did* know more goaded Mum for a reaction, asking why she was there and what the police had told her.

The scenes were shameful. Imagine asking Mum if they thought she was going to identify Lesley, which is exactly what happened. Then, asking her how she felt, when there was nothing to feel, because there was nothing to know and there had been nothing to know or feel for so many months.

They just wanted something on camera. In the years that would follow, I would see this scenario of course so many times on the news that victims' families were pursued in the manner that you would the perpetrators. It was desperately unfair and pretty pointless – as if the media image of people taking pictures of a fleeing car with grieving people inside actually told the story. It was just mean, but we had almost got used to it.

Inside there was nobody. And I say that with double meaning. There were no media, but also there was no Alan – banned from going with Mum, because he was not next of kin.

That was the police fail number three. Rules were rules. What was the purpose of that? I can see none to this day. A dead body is a dead body and the family of that victim surely have the right to identify it with those they love in tow.

Mum's suspicion and trust of the police had now evaporated to the point of no return, from that very first visit on Boxing Day evening when they were pretty much dismissed, to the phone call the previous night. There was always a barrier – almost a power issue. A total lack of compassion, and common sense. A feeling that they were playing God because they could.

Mum had to go alone. As I think of it today, there still seems no need for something so finite. She was poorly through medication and stress. Alan had to wait outside with the police, and who knew anymore if they were leaking stuff, given the speed with which the story appeared the day after Boxing Day and with the press turning up at our door that morning? It just told you two things.

You could not trust anyone and we were always the last to know.

What followed is the low point in existence – and Mum rarely spoke of it again. She expressed it to very few. It is the pit in humanity. I wish I had been there. I am glad I was not. It should not happen to any civilised decent human being.

Mum walked into the room alone – bar the now comforting arm of an officer. Struggling into the light, having been blinded by the light – of the press – she almost keeled over at the sight ahead of her.

On the table laid out were clothes that could only belong to one person.

One pink cardigan, a blue woollen coat, a white blouse and a horrible vile smell.

Mum collapsed vomiting on the floor of the mortuary.

No words were spoken.

It was obvious.

Mum confirmed by her actions and the officer by his silence. Again.

Mum was in pieces – the sterile environment of the mortuary rushing headlong into her maternal instinct and Lesley's abandoned soul, alone in the cold and her finite place of rest.

To one side was a red shoe. It belonged to nobody else. It was my sister's and Mum wanted to take it. A souvenir is the wrong word. Something to cling to. An item that said Lesley. A last contact with her daughter and with my beloved sister.

As bad as her clothing and her little plastic jewellery were, some other items that we had never seen before – futile and tacky and without meaning until now. Next to her were fairground prizes and a gift I had left her. The cheap disposable rubbish that breaks as soon as you leave the event now broke Mum's heart. It represented a gap in our lives and a knowledge of that unknown hour where her free spirit was playing without a care in the world, acquiring stuff that had no meaning, except to a child who felt like they had won the world. The item itself meant nothing – totally devoid of purpose – but now resonated significance. It was something Lesley was proud to have won outside on her own merit, something to bring home with glee, to show off to me and her brothers as though she was standing on her own two feet in life. It was the achievement not the reward and even though insignificant, it was the first piece in a very incomplete jigsaw of the last hours of Lesley.

It is so hard to explain, but when you watched out for your sister as much as I did then you didn't expect to have gaps in your knowledge. It was the same for Mum. She had shaped Lesley. Les was on the way to becoming Mum Part Two and here was something as pointless as a fairground prize that filled us all with panic, which also served no purpose. Lesley was gone and the last object associated with her was something we knew nothing about. It certainly didn't really offer any explanation to the sequence of events either. Whomever she won the fairground tack from was long gone, would have seen the posters and publicity and clearly had nothing to offer as to her abductors. It gave no hope whatsoever, but it reminded you that there was this barren wasteland of knowledge that killed you in not knowing, whilst learning today that she had been taken from us on the barren wasteland of The Moors.

New items like these caused panic and shock in Mum – a ripple effect of thinking 'that is not Lesley's' then realising that of course that it must have been. We now were in that mental space where we had to fill in the gaps and second-guess or assume. That void in concrete information was as painful as the awful facts you could be sure of.

At this stage, Mum had been told little. Still reeling from the contradiction of the call the night before, this was, dare I say it, little more than an identification. Details would surely follow, but even then, it would not be the whole story. Nobody went to court without learning more. That was a long way off. Dealing with the remains of your child and of my sister was enough for one day. You wanted to scream half sentences like 'but how, why, when'. In effect, these were just cries of grief, wailings of pain. If anyone had sat down and explained the facts at this point, it would be too early to take them in – and there were no facts beyond Lesley going missing and Lesley being found. That detail was still to come.

Mum was desperate to get out of there to spend every last minute with Lesley. Once she was gone from the morgue, so was Lesley. But these were just her possessions and this was bad enough.

It was agonising seeing evidence of Lesley, but her body was not with her possessions. I can not describe this as a warm up for what was to follow, or an acclimatisation, but Mum was yet to see Lesley. Was this part of some police protocol that if you rejected the clothes then you didn't have to endure the pain of the body. I don't know. Still to this day, I do not know.

But it was obviously Lesley, underlined by the mistake the night before on the phone. I really cannot understand why Mum had to inspect her possessions and what she was wearing in a state that was barely stable, in that she couldn't really stand, all the time vomiting, and now she had to be led deeper into the mortuary.

Mum always told you she remembered the smell. I have heard that so many times over the years, that a scent can take you back to a memory. You can go years without smelling it and then when you think you catch a whiff of it, it takes you back. So, for Mum, the fear or rubber and formaldehyde would never leave her from this moment. Places like this, I have come to believe, always have an odour that never goes away. Mum said it was freezing too – and would have felt so even in summer. I don't know if that is because it is a morgue or the natural tension that fills your own spirit when you are in there, causing you to shiver uncontrollably. Staff worked there day in day and day out and even though, attuned to the temperature, never seemed fazed by it. I am sure it is a combination of the requirements of the building and that terrible shaking, freezing experience anyone undergoes when the news of death is broken to them. And this, of course, was the most appalling of circumstances.

Mum was still alone, but even if Alan had been by her side, he would have been only as physical support. Mum was long gone, experiencing a desperate solitude, trying to find a unity with Lesley, but herself slipping away into a fragile grief of a day she knew had been coming.

Ahead of her stood a table – another table. Somebody was helping her there – a faceless person, whose name she would never know, was escorting her to the defining moment in her life. It was awful that the clinical nature of rules and regulation and trained staff meant that such a moment had to be shared – and amongst those who were just doing their job.

Between Mum and Lesley lay a green sheet. You could see how small Les was by how little was needed to cover her in her entirety. Discreetly, the right side of her body and face were specifically concealed as if to alert Mum not to try to look. We concluded that she was badly beaten. There was at least some sensitivity. In the moment Mum didn't really think about. She only pieced it together long after the event. You don't have rational thought process at moments like this. Your mind is so detached from anything close to the truth that by the time you realise why, you are never in that position again in life to return to the body. You have no desire to ever go there again, but the problem is that the scene replays in your mind every day for the rest of your life, and the more information you acquire, whether through rumour or fact, then the more you dream that you are pulling back the cover over the right side of Lesley's face, grasping at a scene in time that is no longer real. You know the truth, but the dislocation between the moment that Mum was there and the subsequent knowledge meant she was always there, craving an alternative ending, wishing she could pack the sheet in full.

Instead, she saw her swollen lips – the sole marker as to what she had been through that Mum was allowed to view.

The slightest glimpse of life, when there was nothing but death, derailed Mum's emotions from a wailing painful yelling cry to a sorrowful, heartbroken sob. Grief does come in stages and with different tones. The cycle of pain stooped at anger and broke down in full at tears.

Then a blow that Mum would never forget.

Her whole demeanour softened. Mum began to mumble.

She couldn't hear the hushed words of the staff around her as she leant forward to touch Lesley's curly hair. It was a natural instinct and act that she had done so many times, with her setting off for school, or indeed the fair. It was a mother's hand reaching for her child. Then suddenly the echo of the morgue resonated:

'No, you can't touch her,' she was told.

This was the pain of the moment. A dead child, my deceased sister – and Mum so close but so far, unable to connect for the last time, but why? I have asked myself so many times over the years and, of course, I understand about contaminating evidence, but the fact of the matter was that, despite the officers putting us under a scrutinising pressure, and an intense analysis of Alan's character at the house, there was no way anybody thought that Mum had anything to do with this, so surely a gentle flick of Les's hair or a holding of her hand could not upset the medical process. I know rules are rules, but if the science was that good – even then – it was clear whose fingerprints were whose and in an area of pre-DNA analysis, there can not be any chance of Mum tampering with evidence. She just wanted to hold her little girl one more time. One final time.

Of course, as a family we were thrust into this situation. We did not know how the law worked and never expected to be asked to give statements or identify clothing and bodies, so for Mum to be spurned the chance to be with Lesley was really incomprehensible for a simple family who had never had anything to do with the media or the police.

That manifested itself in Mum's reaction, staring at the officer and then vomiting uncontrollably into the sink in the room. I don't know if that sink was there for staff to wash hands or because my Mum's reaction was standard. All I do understand is that tipped her over and the hushed sobbing of seeing Lesley's body returned to the growling pain of anger.

And yet nobody asked her to confirm that it was Lesley. Not once. I have no idea what to make of this. Obviously, Mum's lack of words and physical reactions said it all, but we were dealing with an officious organisation who even then liked to tick boxes and be regimented in their stance.

It seems an odd detail to recall – unless Mum did not hear it and has no recollection – that in one of the biggest cases in British legal history, nobody officially asked her if this was Lesley. I think if they had, the damage was done anyway. Mum was spent of emotions that a simple yes would not have tilted her either way. It would not have been the moment she lost it. She was way past that.

I think, out of courtesy, no question was asked. This was all about formalities. They knew it was Lesley, without Mum being there or confirming. Very simply, how many cases have there been over the years when someone has been asked to confirm the identity of someone deceased, only to send the police back to the drawing board? It is an almost certain scenario – the end game – that when you get that call, they are ahead of you and know the answer. For those who enact the law and document it, it is the final sheet of paper. For those who attend, it is the first step on the road to acceptance. There is no such thing as recovery. And there remains a long way to go.

Mum always told me she thought they were actually compassionate and that is why they did not need to ask if it was Lesley. I wonder how many times that has happened. For me, I only cared about Lesley. But was this the norm?

It was a terrible task to have to oversee and this was probably as grim as it ever got. A dead body was a dead body, but even then, in the 1960s this was and probably remains the most graphic scenario for those staff.

I don't know if the brandy was standard, but Mum was offered it and duly obliged. Mum could not keep it down, as much as she needed that drink, together with further medication. They tried again and this time she managed it as she was ushered away. Despite the compassion appearing to be available, she was soon gestured to move on with assistance and it was over in a flash – a sensation you would both want to have linger and disappear in an instant. It was finite and it was painful. It was agonisingly cruel as an experience, but one that you wanted to prolong, knowing that it was the last time.

It is so hard to explain that paradox between needing to get the hell out of there and craving to stay one more minute more, because you can never get it back after.

Mum sensed that, shrugging off the warden's arm and begging to look at Lesley one more time, as he led her in the direction of the door. Mum needed one more look. Les had always been pretty quiet and now she was still forever. Mum needed to see that for the last time. Lesley was dead.

She could see with her own eyes, but she needed to see again. There was still a connection and she needed to savour it until it could be no more.

She lent over the body to kiss Lesley goodbye, but a gentle hand on her shoulder told her no. Then she was reduced to all but begging for a piece of Lesley's hair only to be refused again. Nobody knew where to look. Mum could take no more, collapsing to her knees and vomiting just to the side of Lesley's body.

There was to be no more. This was the cue for the wardens to intervene – several almost dragging Mum to the door, where Alan met her as she desperately tried to turn to see Lesley one last time. One final glimpse was all she wanted. They had covered Lesley once more in the green sheet. It was too late.

Chapter 10

'Is it?' I asked.

I had been sat on the stairs with my brothers, waiting and hoping, just praying for one stroke of fortune that would reverse this awful ten months in our life.

Even my questions had now changed. They simply said that all hope was gone.

It had been horrendous outside of the morgue – no room for privacy. Mum was forced to leave in the undignified manner of having a coat thrown over her head – the world's media hustling and jockeying for position, thrusting them into a sea of flashbulbs.

They asked the same question – was it Lesley? Mum said nothing until she got in the car and when she arrived home, it was the same again – the coat over her head after a high-speed chase and more photographers and reporters. There was nothing to say and where was the merit in a woman whose face was covered? In the moment of her greatest grief in life, Mum said she felt like the criminal, ashamed to show her face, but for no reason other than it showed remorse and pain that very few would ever experience. It was normally those in the dock who were buried under a blanket. Now, it was Mum protected from the glare of the media for her own good. They all wanted that shot, but truthfully nobody wanted to see that frail broken tear-stained face. It was one of the grim sensations in life that moments, meant to be so private, had to be so public.

'Is it?' I sobbed again to Mum as she finally made it in the house.

She just nodded.

And I fell into her arms.

'It's all my fault,' I told her again. 'I should never have let Les go to the fair. I let her down.'

I was angry. Months of stomach-churning fear and doubt, being unable to express myself just exploded into a moment of rage. I had never had an outburst like this, but then I had never found myself in a scenario like this, and I just flew into a rage. Something triggered it. I think even then I understood the lack of dignity at Mum coming in under a coat. I didn't understand how the press worked, except that I had seen them at all hours from all angles in the last few months, but your instinct for your Mum kicks in when you see such an undignified entrance.

She was certainly juggling roles – the media story, the grieving individual fleeing the mob, but mostly the mother who had to switch in an instant from looking after her own physical well-being and self-preservation against the uncontrollable lens into our house. There was little time for her to prepare words or the way she would break the news to us. She had no choice but to go from fugitive back to our Mum and break the news that meant that our hearts fled our souls forever.

It was left to Alan, or rather he just found the words.

'Lesley has gone to the angels,' he told us calmly.

It was the first time I heard this phrase.

In time, I came to hear it over and over again as the years passed – in various contexts, as other children went missing in the news and famous faces left us too soon.

But they seemed perfect words now as Alan spoke them for the first time. If there was any comfort in this terrible story, it was at least consoling that she had gone up above – just to a place that resonated peace as a noun. Where was the pain and grief in being at one with the angels? It just sounded restful – a calmness that she deserved and it sounded finite. She was safe. Finally. Nobody, however evil, could infiltrate the sphere of peace around the angels, and Lesley was well and truly tucked up inside it. She was floating in the clouds with a soundtrack of stillness trickling by. Alan found the words alright and it was the best way to explain it to my younger brothers.

I looked at Mum again and we hugged. Closure is an awful word and only something that can be attempted in time, but in this moment, it drew the metaphorical curtain on an utterly appalling ten months. At home too, we blacked out the windows against the peering eyes of the press wanting their story.

In time, I have come to learn much more about the media and how celebrity manipulate press for PR. Here we were, exactly in that situation, but through no choice of our own. Of course, we did not crave media attention, but we certainly needed it, particularly from those quiet skeleton staff days of Boxing Day when Lesley went missing.

It was in fact the same scenario as a footballer's wife, posing in a bikini, in agreement with the paparazzi to further their latest lingerie, perfume or charity for their own ego and to swell their own coffers.

We had been guilty of that same lure – the need to feed the baying pack – but obviously our cause was a moral one. We just wanted Lesley back.

So, on reflection, it was totally understandable that we had to draw our curtains to the constant blinking of the cameras. I will not say that they had every right to be there, but I think in the trade-off, they probably felt justified.

At this time, Mum looked haggard and it was certainly not for now, but this moment must have slept in her subconscious. She was not a publicity-seeker, but over the next few years, she would slug it out with the best of them in public. She somehow learned from the power of the media from this moment. It caused her immense stress and grief, living everything out in public, but in time, through circumstances everyone wishes could have been averted, empowered her too. That was later.

Alan had managed to dress it up as though she had gone to the place that we had found in our dreams. *I* knew that if I had been well, she would be here today. I was grateful that he had found the language that almost glossed over the moment, and even for me, it sounded peaceful, but the truth remained that it was my fault.

I was mature enough to understand this window dressing, but I had been there – or rather hadn't – and yes, I still was not really sufficiently life experienced enough to know death. I had not lost anyone close to me before, nor indeed anybody at all that I can recall. I did not comprehend what death meant. She had gone to 'heaven' because she was an angel, and she was with them, but I did not have any concept of what it all meant. I was straddling my maturity – living through it, seeing its devastating effect, but caught in the middle with no comprehension. The only thing I can say, hand on heart, is that it was finite.

In time too, when my seven-year-old granddaughter would ask me what happened to Lesley, I would simply reply that 'she just died'. You sense they know something. They work out who bad people are.

History repeated itself, but history never left you. We were now part of that history, but it would manifest itself down the generations to come in my own family. You found yourself giving innocent answers to the next generation – the narrative was inherited and outlived you. So, when Alan had explained about the angels, the next question was whether Lesley was happy there. She was, he assured us.

It pacified. It radiated that calm, which being with the angels had already suggested. It was an incredible situation in that the worst was over. The worst had long been over, but had just been hanging in the unknown. Now, it was confirmed and for that night alone, it settled the mind. We *could* go to bed knowing that Lesley was with the angels and for the first time in an eternity, we could have those falsely-sold sweet dreams.

I know I went to bed and in the night and mid-sleep was giggling to myself. I kept hearing the phrase 'just leave me alone'. I was back straddling that maturity line. My mind, still confused, had settled – into a curious relaxed demeanour, when I hadn't really dreamt in months and certainly not anything less than sinister thoughts.

I do not know what this represents except the giggling was the fun my sis and I had together – an emotion I had never re-visited since her abduction. In my night-time thoughts, I think I flew up and visited the angels, checked she was just fine and then came crashing back down to earth, realising the pain of it all – hence the 'just leave me alone'. I know that my mind tried to visualise her death and attempted to get as close as I possibly could to narrow that gap in my knowledge in the timeline from when she left the house to…when, who knows?

Sadly, as we all reached this state of acceptance at the end of the longest of days, in which a constant procession of friends, neighbours and relatives passed by again to offer sympathy and assistance, despite anyone actually telling them the truth, other than the media, we did manage to go bed with a sliver of peace.

Anguish had subsided but pain comes in stages. We were now on to the next level of grief, but it was not a progression upwards. It was most certainly downwards. There was, after all, nothing these visitors could have done or do now. We would be grateful for their words, but they felt empty. They glazed past us, trotted out from the bottom of their hearts, but to a stunned audience who had lived every moment of this and had not been able to re-join the story as they had. Time had separated our well-wishers from the daily and nightly pain in our heads. They could at least have a *time-out*. When they came to our house that day, they had been able to check in and out of our story. For us, it was a constant.

For Mum, there no checking in or out, she was overcome with fatigue and grief and Alan had to call for the doctor once more, dosing her up with a heavy sedative. She was oblivious now to almost everything – you couldn't escape the press outside, but she was so groggy that it became possible. In her head, just one image of the morgue kept coming back to her, returning her to her senses, before she drifted out again. There was no turning the clock back and getting past the moment. The hands of time would fall regularly at this point until the day Mum herself died.

For me, the point of reference was different – close to a year before, on the Boxing Day with Lesley going to the fair.

But for Mum, no amount of preparing for the worst and in your head having that small amount of hope, but common sense eroding belief every day that there was any hope. Nothing can replace that moment when you see your own child on a cold slab in a mortuary. You think you can foresee all the possible scenarios in the period of waiting and hoping – none include identifying your child.

The truth was that if today was the day that unravelled all our worst fears, it was about to get much grimmer. The discovery of Lesley's body remains a finite moment in our story. It is a definite end. What was inevitable was that we were now about to face the harsh details of how Les had ended up there. Dealing with the shock of the end was horrific and her body clearly said pain at the hands of evil.

We were soon to learn two things – just how evil, and that her abduction may have been a conclusion, not closure to us, but it actually fell in the middle of a much more complicated plot.

Chapter 11

The police had become aware of three victims. There was no comfort in learning that this was a shared experience. Dealing with Lesley's body was hard enough, but they were way ahead.

On 23 November, 1963, and thirteen whole months before Lesley, a twelve-year-old boy had been approached at a market in Ashton-under-Lyne in the suburbs of Manchester, and had been offered a lift home in a hired Ford Anglia. He was sold the ride on two counts – that his parents would be worried and that there was a bottle of sherry waiting at the end. John got into the car. Inside the car were Myra Hindley and Ian Brady.

Brady told John that they would have to make a detour for the alcohol at his house, and a second stop on the moors to search for a glove that Hindley had lost there – presumably a clue to previous as yet unknown offences.

Whilst Hindley waited in the car, Brady led John away and sexually assaulted him, trying in the process to slit his throat, before strangling him to death with string.

Lesley was next. She had been standing by one of the rides. They had pretended to drop some shopping near her, once they had established she was alone and then asked her to help carry some of the packages to the car. From there they took her to their house, gagging her and forcing her to pose for photographs, before raping and killing her. It seems that Lesley had been taken to Saddleworth Moors the next morning, buried naked with her clothes to one side in a very shallow grave.

Then, it seemed, there was nothing. Perhaps the timing of Lesley's disappearance over the festive period cooled them off or they had satisfied their sick appetites for the time being.

It was the murder of Edward Evans on 6 October 1965 which turned out to be the breakthrough moment. He was much older at 17, and was unfortunate enough to be in Brady's path at Manchester Central Station when he was coerced back to their home.

Brady beat him to death with an axe. 16, Wardle Brook Avenue in Hattersley had now become of one those infamous houses in the history of British crime.

When we later discovered that this was where Brady and Hindley had been living, our worlds sunk even more. When Mum had moved after Lesley's disappearance, unbeknownst to us we had actually moved closer to them. We were but a stone's throw away.

There are two significant moments in the sad killing of Edward Evans – one is the railway station, the other is that it was witnessed.

Hindley had a sister called Maureen, who had married David Smith. Smith himself had a violent criminal past, dating back to the age of eleven, and the family disapproved. He, though, saw something in Brady to the point of idolisation. Brady courted his friendship in return – much to the irritation of Hindley.

At the Brady house that night, Hindley was sent to fetch her brother-in-law and on the signal of a flashing light was to knock on the door for the 'wine bottles'. Brady led Smith into the kitchen and left him there.

Shortly after, Smith heard a scream and Hindley called for help – at which point Smith found Brady on the lounge floor bashing Edward with an axe and then strangling him with electrical chord. Brady had injured himself in the fight and needed Smith's help to carry the body to the car, but for now had to leave it in the spare room, arranging to dispose of it the next evening.

However, it is at this moment that everything turned and was able to give John Kilbride's family and ours some sort of conclusion.

Smith told Hindley's sister, Maureen, who insisted they call the police. Once subservient and in awe, Smith now turned Brady in and placed that call.

On 7 October, the Superintendent of Cheshire Police arrived at Wardle Brook Avenue, concealing his uniform and, met by Hindley at the door, asked to speak to Brady, who had been writing a note to his boss to say that he sprained his ankle and would not be in for work. The Superintendent, Bob Talbot, explained that he was investigating gun-related violence the previous evening, which Hindley denied, allowing the police to look around the house.

When they came to the room where Edward's body was stored, the door was locked. Hindley said the key was at work and when the officer offered to drive her there to get it, Brady just told her to open it.

Inside was Edward. Brady was arrested on suspicion of murder, telling the police that 'Eddie and I had a row and the situation got out of hand.'

Hindley was not arrested, but insisted on accompanying Brady to the station. On questioning, she merely said there had been an accident and was allowed to go home to return the next day.

In the days that followed, she remained free, even turning up at work, asking to be fired, with the sole purpose of claiming benefits and in the process burning in an ashtray some documents belonging to Brady, believed to be plans for robberies.

On 11 October, Hindley was charged as an accessory to murder. At this stage that was only of Edward Evans.

During interrogation, Brady tried to rope Smith in, claiming that the two had murdered Edward Evans together. Smith, in turn told police that Brady had ordered him to return anything which may incriminate him – 'dodgy books' for example, and Brady then packed these into suitcases. Smith claimed to be unaware of the contents of the suitcases, but did mention casually, without any comprehension of why, that Brady liked his railway stations. Obviously, these were a magnet for people of all ages – student types, like Edward – plus you could also blend in with the crowd. And this is the second significant detail, because on 15 October, British

66

Transport Police searched the left luggage at Manchester's main station.

At the house, they found exercise books in which the name John Kilbride had been scribbled. This really was the key to unravelling that there was more than one victim. They also found many photos from Saddleworth Moor and, on that discovery, the search of the Moors began.

The police were assisted by an eleven-year-old named Pat Hodges, who had somehow survived being taken there and was able to indicate a likely route and stop-off points.

On 16 October, they found the bone of an arm sticking out of the peat. The instinct was that it belonged to John, since it had been his name in the books near the photos at the house. But it wasn't John. They had found Lesley.

Mum had been up there the previous day, but hadn't seen them discover a body. This sequence of events goes some way to explaining the phone call that told us it *wasn't* Lesley.

But they found Lesley first, just off the A635 and then five days later, a badly decomposed body that was John – only identifiable through his clothing, it was in such a bad state. There were now three when they had only known of Edward and suspected there might be John. Their gut was that there were more, but essentially it was John they were looking for.

By November, the search for more bodies was called off as winter set in and dark nights arrived, but it was the discovery in the railway station that caused the most distress.

Chapter 12

Alan was the first to be aware of the tape. I have never listened to it. Once was far more than enough for Mum. He handled much of the new information and selectively passed it on. He probably would have avoided telling Mum at all about it if it weren't for the fact that the police wanted to confirm it was Lesley, and that it would mostly be played at trial. There were no good scenarios here, but avoiding it in public was the lesser of two evils – and these were two evils.

Hyde Police had given him the word, off the record, when he went for Lesley's possessions. And then an officer came around with a big folder under his arm, asking Mum to formally identify Lesley from the photos found at the left luggage.

How many more identifications? And these were awful. Mum took moments before she found the briefest of seconds to look down at the bundle. It was only now that this horrid truth emerged.

Lesley was naked, with a scarf rammed into her mouth and tied to the back of her neck to cause maximum damage with any movement. There were others too – one forcing my sister into a mock prayer, bent over on a chair.

Mum was delirious in mental agony, already unstable with the Valium and now seeing the real fear and torment in Lesley's eyes. It was the eyes that told the story – never mind the nudity and the ties. You can always see fear in people's look and it was there. Beyond terrified.

Mum collapsed to the floor, a shaking wreck, as the officer asked her to formally identify Lesley. Even Alan was in tears – and these were not the worst images. They had been specifically chosen sensitively, so that only meant one thing. You did not want to see the others.

The images were pornographic. She was ten and had yet to discover her body. We all used to tease her about how shy she was. Now these animals had made her take her clothes off. She would have been terrified in her mind, long before they had brought pain to her through torture. I know this was the moment Mum really wanted to die herself, to swap places with Lesley and take the pain away by taking the pain for her. She hadn't slept with worry in the last ten months, apart from when the medication kicked in. Now even they were failing her. I could hear her most nights wailing in torment – the graphic nature of the images having the strength to knock dead the hallucinating powers of the drugs. These images had taken her to the next level – down to the next level, if that was at all possible.

And after the photos came the audio. The day after the visit to the house, Mum was summoned to Hyde Police Station again. Alan knew why, but had shielded it from Mum. But it only slowly dawned on her why. There was a tape recorder on the desk – as there often was. But they were no longer suspects. Mum didn't see what was coming.

She bit the officer's head off just before he pressed play when he told her that he too had a daughter. No, Mum *had* a daughter. He still *has* one. Sometimes people made things worse when they didn't know what to say. They meant well, but there was nothing anyone could say. Then silence also became uncomfortable.

The tape began.

The previous day's images were gruesome, but they were literally stills. They were a moment. Hearing a voice was worse. It makes Lesley almost alive again. As though you can reach out and feel her. The sound of someone's voice, who you know to be deceased, dislocates time. If Valium did not disorientate you then hearing someone dead seemingly living left you slipping between agonising realities, feigning that belief that they were still there, even though the audio was clearly a point of no return.

Mum told me that the recording must have been fifteen minutes maximum. But perhaps she really didn't know.

Fear rose in her for Lesley and for herself when the tape hissed into action. It was never going to be anything but utterly appalling. This was more misery. This was not ever going to be Lesley in her prime – some audio they had found and were leaving as a keepsake of happier times. No, this was going to be brutal.

In short, it was going to bring the pictures to life – and therefore to death.

The incidental detail will forever leave its imprint. Mum could hear the strains of Little Drummer Boy in the background – a reminder out of context that this all happened at Christmas time and that time of year was shattered forever. It was a cruel detail to hear, something so peaceful and spiritual, so associated with a magical time as a pre-cursor to the violence and pain that would follow and from audio over image, we gain one defying detail and symbol of brutality that we can gain nowhere else.

Tone.

Brady bellowed to Lesley twice, asking her name.

It was nasty. It was power. It was control. You had seen similar scenes of interrogators in war films, but never ever addressing a child.

You could now hear the terror in Lesley's responses too. That quivering stumbling voice – a direct contrast to the menace of Brady and providing an unwelcome soundtrack to the pictures Mum had to endure the previous day. Now, they matched. The muted nightmares Mum had been having in the night, overcoming the drugs, now had a voice.

Mum said that one sentence, more than any other, epitomised the fear of the moment.

Lesley had attempted to answer and got her name wrong. Who had ever done that in life? It seemed the one thing everybody could be sure they were certain of.

'Lesley Ann Weston,' she had answered through tears.

She had, of course, been Downey but was way past the name change being an obstacle. There had never been one. She had just become Lesley Ann West, even though all the media was reporting her as Downey after her disappearance.

70

Mum said the music drove her mad, but just like the officer before the moment, he pressed play, so did the silence. When faced with audio where nothing is happening, but there is clearly a live scene, you make up in your head what is going on. From what Mum knew at that point, it could have been undressing her or the preparation of something to gag Lesley.

It was the latter.

'Please don't make me take my clothes off,' Lesley had asked meekly, barely audible against Brady's power machine.

And then the line that destroyed Mum.

'Let me go home to Mummy.'

Then you could hear Hindley on the tape, telling Lesley, in no uncertain terms, that a hiding was coming if she spoke again.

It didn't really matter. The hiding was coming either way. If you can reduce it to those terms.

With an innocence that only came with Lesley's age, she protested once more – though she was so softly spoken through fear that you couldn't call it a protest, as she voiced her concern that Mum would be cross for not coming home straight from the fair.

That told you everything. None of us were ever late. That is why Mum was adamant that first time that evening when she went to the police station. It had been drilled into us and it was just something that we didn't do.

And then the same officer, who had been round to Brady's house, rapidly slammed his hand down on the tape to stop it. It was over. It felt like a dream sequence, despite the voices adding real life.

He had to ask Mum once more to confirm that it was Lesley. Nothing needed to be said – except for the record. They had played her perhaps a minute or two. It clearly got worse. Much, much worse. Mum was spared the pain that Lesley was not. She had seen the images of what followed. Now, she didn't need that soundtrack.

But what she was well aware of from the duration of the recording was that this was a planned, drawn-out, meticulous execution and she had heard Hindley's voice for the first time. Realising that Brady was a psychopath was something in time that people came to understand. But Mum could never get over that another woman could do that to a little girl.

Chapter 13

It is Tuesday 26 October, 1965. Lesley is to be buried today. I don't know how we got here. Again. You drift in a trance towards the day. It all happens so fast, but you need to be guided. One minute, Mum is on the Moors, only to receive a call to say it is a boy and not Lesley; the next you wake up and the press know and they are at your door. Then you are trying to cling to the last moments of Lesley, through the process of identifying her battered and bruised body and then you are bombarded with horrific pictures and sounds that even your worst nightmares could never have conjured before. Then it is over and you are here.

We found the funeral prepared for us. Not even Alan had the strength to do much more than oversee the arrangements. Thankfully, so many people around us came good. Their passing interest and momentary concern was way better than curtain-twitching. They had stayed the course and the same mentality that had funded Lesley's posters now manifested itself in Miles Platting and Charnley Walk. Somehow the community had funded the costs. The doorbell hadn't stopped ringing. The arrival of wreaths was endless. Many ended up in bedrooms or neighbours' gardens. We had uncles, aunts and friends staying too. Nothing prepared you for this.

And still, to the last, we were denied Lesley. We did not awake on that morning to find her there waiting. We had not spent the previous evening just looking at her one more time. All the moments Mum had been with Lesley since her death were fleeting and all for police procedure. There had been no time allowed to linger.

I have no idea how the previous day would have turned out if we had been left with Lesley's body. What do you do? Do you have a million last conversations? Do you have the angry one, followed by the gentle one, interspersed with the times you laughed and the times you fought that seemed so needless now? Do you approach the coffin so many times, grabbing every moment, or do you go out? Is it that you seize every last moment you can or is enough *enough*? We probably needed the distraction of visitors, but either way you cannot discount the emotional energy spent on days like these. It was the same old story of endless trips to the kettle or something stronger as we drowned in goodwill messages – all the time the police at our door and the press kept just more than a stone's throw away. Heaven only knows what our neighbours must have thought when we moved in. I doubt we had been allowed to do it discreetly, even though some months had passed since Lesley's disappearance. Now they could see the full extent of the siege that we had been under previously. I hadn't worked for the previous eight days. I just wanted it over.

Mum tells a story that I do not recall – that Alan had busied himself with the mundane, cracking on with painting and doing jobs and because of the smell, had left the front door open, which of course opened us up potentially to the world's media who mostly stood and waited.

But it wasn't the press who came up to the house. Two massive white unaccompanied dogs made their way from nowhere without fuss into the hall of the house. Mum and Alan stared at the dogs, who turned around. And off they went through the house and out the back door in the kitchen and onto the fields out the back. Then they disappeared onto the moorland and were never seen again and when Mum and Alan asked around, nobody knew anything about them, nor claimed to be their owners.

Mum thought it might be some sort of sign. Who could ever know? Some things just remain unexplained.

I remember, by the time nightfall came, that the house became quite quiet after everyone had been trying to keep themselves busy during the day. Nervous energy and the need to fill the air with conversation and tea plateaued by the evening, as if everyone knew that they had helped themselves get this far, but now the real challenge lay ahead. We knew what lay ahead tomorrow. And we had to get through the night and the following day. We had to bury our Lesley. We thought we knew what lay ahead. But in reality, we had no idea at all.

***

Mum was up early. I remember that much. She was trying to hold it together after another night, halfway between out for the count with Diazepam and unable to sleep with stress, flashbacks and a sickly stomach. There was no mindset of once it was out of the way we could all get on with our lives. That is why the whole closure conversation never happens. Other people talk like that. We couldn't see beyond the next few hours and when we would get there all we would find was a pain that we had learnt to cope with, but would never go away.

Of course, as we woke that morning our lives split into two paths. Ahead was our day – Lesley's day, as Mum put it. But then there was everyone else's day, which we hadn't even considered. We knew the press would be waiting, but we had not for a moment considered playing a role in anything other than our own lives.

We had seen it all before so many times, or so we thought. Now, there was nothing like this. Rightly so, we had been preparing our thoughts and ourselves within our four walls, but for many, the real story was out there and it was us. We had been staring at the inside of this house for so long, and in the last 24 hours, what felt like forever, and now, whilst we had become accustomed to the glare of the lens, we realised the whole world *was* watching us.

Whilst we remained in the house, they couldn't see what we were just about clinging to. We still just about had each other. The morning came and gave us maybe an hour, perhaps two – I can't really have any sense of time. Little was said. Props took over, like the boiling of the kettle again or finding a window to stare out of. Still people came by. Yet more flowers. They meant well. They might have helped. When you look back you don't really remember who came or

75

what they said. You just remember the constant – and that was the doorbell ringing and its opening and shutting. Of all the people who came I only recall my Dad and his four brothers.

It had already felt a long morning by the time the moment came to leave. I had never looked so smart. Tommy and Brett were not to come. I think they went to a friend's house for the day, but there was no doubt that, even though they didn't fully comprehend, they knew...

By 10 am it was time to go.

A fifteen-minute drive took an hour. It was a route we knew inside out. Trinity Church was where Lesley had adored Sunday School. But now, it was unrecognisable. Those serene Sixties Sundays where families were together and the shops were shut in streets that remained still and quiet, was how we knew this road and this journey. Now, it was almost unrecognisable. The post box on the corner, the newsagent where Mum got the paper, and even street lamps that towered above us all were lost in the masses. I say this with no glee, but every vantage point was taken.

Those whom we know, and others who shared our grief because of the tragic nature of the story and because Lesley could have been their own daughter, were just faces in the crowd. Everyone went to that fair and by now Brady and Hindley's web was shown to be far flung. Well-wishers understood the random nature of Lesley's selection and in time they would learn its cynical planning. As we left Ancoats Lane in circumstances that would never ever come again, I heard people shouting my name from the street. Then by the time, we passed the hospital, I had tuned out.

For now, friend and stranger were unidentifiable in the throng several rows back on the pavements and high above from wherever they could pay their respects. I passed friends from school, and those supporting Mum and Alan, but I knew none of them on that day, nor could I make them out. Blurred vision had kicked in. I could feel them from inside the funeral car almost making us claustrophobic as they lined the streets, but they didn't really exist as individuals. And they came with no soundtrack either. A mid-level murmur that was neither silence nor cries for justice, just a hum from the street – thousands of broken incomplete sentences that tailed away as the emotion of the day meant that people just couldn't find the words.

In the procession it was worse. We had barely found the language to express ourselves in the last ten months and now only silence prevailed. What was there to say? Almost everyone attends a funeral at some point, so you probably understand that mute state, but almost none of us become a public spectacle sharing the grief with the world, yet trance-like so your grief is not shared, just broadcast globally. It is a different kind of share. In that hearse, you don't feel the pressure of the occasion – that is a phrase for other people. You simply turn off the soundtrack and the only visuals that you register are initially when wreaths on Bowden Close merged into bright colours that defied the crispness and coldness of the season. Inside the car, nobody was hysterical, just sullen-faced and tear-stained.

I see today those crowds of people that I couldn't really identify on the day. It has replayed in my mind often, of course. I still don't make out individuals, but I see the mass and with the benefit of time, I see photos from time to time and the magnitude never leaves you. Pictures of the day – you must understand – are not items that we get out and look at with nostalgia. They mostly come down from the loft when researchers make polite enquiries or as our kids and then their kids became older, and the time arrives to have this conversation about what they had been born into.

Flanked by police out-riders, the most distressing car journey I would ever take arrived over an hour later and when we emerged, the crowds were even greater. The slowness of every detail was painstaking. The choreography of a funeral was at somebody else's discretion. Getting to the church so slowly, then having to wait for the door to be held open whilst waiting on the signal from the police, but all the time looking for Mum and Alan in the car ahead, left me uncertain. I was looking to be led.

I had become accustomed to the flashing bulbs and regular crowds outside our house. That was serene by comparison. It was, after all, a scrum of professionals – journalists creating a frenzy, but ultimately in control to get that picture. This was now police, public, and press, not trying to cause mayhem like that swell at a pop concert or a political rally, but simply just the surge of people that nobody could have predicted, leaving those in charge powerless to control the scenes.

I felt myself being almost sucked out of the car under the chaperone of the police and one of the undertakers. The silence had gone. Speed and soundtrack returned and, in an instant, we had to get inside. Lesley's coffin was already entering the church – the building and routine we knew so well now seemed like a place we hardly recognised at all. Mum was struggling and, with Alan on one side and the Reverend on the other, she entered a church where almost everyone was already seated. I had no comparisons to pull from memory. This was my first funeral. It ripped me to pieces to have everybody turn their eyes towards Mum and then further cut me open when I could see fully the size of Lesley's coffin now stationery at the front of the church.

Of course, she was smaller than me, but the box carrying her to her final place of rest was devastatingly petite. I think anyone who has buried children will say that this moment hits them and I know it took Mum by shock, given that we had not had her body at ours the previous night.

I recall very little of the service, except that Reverend Ford began by saying that 'one of our flock is missing' and that Lesley's seat in the choir was left vacant and that symbolism spoke as much as any a word in the next hour. Some poor chorister would in time have to sit where our Les had sat many a time. Except now she was not there and nor would she be coming back.

The service felt long, weighted out with all the religious protocol. When I look back, I realise how few words are spoken of the individual at a funeral. Amidst the songs, the pauses and the readings, a mere handful of words is about Lesley. I knew no different. You don't expect to be going to funerals at this age. You don't really know what they are. They are just something that happen to older people – other people's grandparents – at the same place you go to Sunday School. The venue is the same and it looks sad, but it is not something you will have to deal with any time soon.

And of course, even if you are ready for someone's death and in time, I could see my Mum's coming from a long way out, there is nothing that prepares you for that racing through the gears, that propelling at speed of the mundane of normal life to the utter chaos of a loved one leaving you. It is the one given in this world – that we all depart – yet none of us have ever mastered a survival technique or a coping strategy.

When you are barely a teenager, and you feel the guilt and the responsibility of your role in this, and you throw in the media speculation and press intrusion and the chaos of a poorly mother, an absent father and two younger brothers, there is simply no knowledge of what to expect.

I glazed over through proceedings. If I say I wanted it over that is an assumption I make with hindsight, and under the pretence that I comprehended what was going on. It was all background noise. It was somebody else's event. It wasn't ours and it was barely Lesley's. I recognised Mum and Alan, of course, and the faces at the front of the church in the congregation. But it was a soundtrack – on in the background. We just drifted heavily by.

Mum sobbed throughout. I bowed my head down. Maybe I wasn't mature enough to ball my eyes out. As a kid, a cut knee or a rollicking for being late might have set me off, but they were childlike tears. I sat by Mum, for the last few months a wreck on drugs, false hope and soul-destroying grief, and watched her break down as you would expect in front of everybody. I didn't yet have that depth to replicate. Instead, it rendered me mute. I think that defines the child-adult disparity of emotion. I knew to cry, I think, but Mum was uncontrollable. When Reverend Ford announced the 23rd Psalm, which was Lesley's favourite, Mum lost whatever was left in her.

Who could think of other children of that age who shared favourite passages from The Bible and that it was so widely known that Lesley adored this? That resonated, if not at the time, but years after, and remains a thought to be cherished to this day that, religion or no religion, she had *religious* values and in that a code of conduct that she took from Mum and she expressed in this welcoming community every Sunday. She knew how to behave and the difference between right and wrong and I think this cut Mum deep when that notion of such purity had run headlong into such evil. I will not judge Lesley's story outside of its context, but I don't see this community today. Despite the pain and regrets, of which I carry the burden to this day, I am bursting with pride that my little sister held such ideals and others saw them in her – even at that age. It wasn't that nobody had a bad word to say about her. Everybody had kindness to express, in that moment and before and after. I took nothing religious from this as the Psalm was read out. Tranquillity filled the church. Mum's sobbing isolated the soundtrack, interrupted by the throng uttering Amen, reverberating from outside, where the demand had been so intense that speakers had been erected to enable the public occasion. They were all just words in the background to me. I remained physically present but spiritually, I had departed too.

Mum and I were expressing the same grief from different ages and mine paralysed me. Me – rabbit in the headlights, staring nowhere without focus, and Mum – removed from any context of environment, except for it bringing the final outpouring from her. She didn't hear the words or the occasion either, sobbing along in delay but somehow – and it is an impossible emotion to express – the ambience of other people gathering in a religious format to

80

honour, remember, commemorate, mourn and say goodbye to Lesley brought her almost year-long numbness to the fore. Those days and weeks when she paced round the house or slumped in a chair or had to be helped to bed heavily medicated all arrived at this, and with it, her raw emotion bled and bled.

There had to be an end to this hour of agony. Maybe it was longer. An official record will detail that, but I can tell you that there is no clock on eternity and we were staring into that abyss.

Anyone who has attended a funeral will know that feeling that you sense it is ending. There is also nothing worse that tears a gaping hole in your heart when you bury someone younger than you or whom you know should be there instead of you. That is how I felt.

The Reverend Ford uttered words that I did not hear at the time, but have learned since.

'He leadeth me beside quiet waters…he restoreth my soul.'

It seems some religious justification, a mantra to make you accept that Lesley has gone to a better place. I didn't understand it then and I am not sure about it now. If there is a divine authority above then this would not have happened, and the notion of going to a better place is much trotted out, but it ignores one counter point of view – that this remains a suitable religious argument for those who justify the innocent being taken. Lesley was too young to experience a better place. She had barely graced the surface of this one.

And those who were still here took life a little less for granted and lined the streets silently as we left with the Reverend alongside Lesley.

We didn't have the lives then that we do now, but my goodness me, we valued the simple things and, on that day, everybody was grateful for what they had – family, peace, security, humility, modesty, and life – uncorrupted by today's trappings and all action 24-hour society that today would have seen Lesley with a mobile phone and her own YouTube channel. Those values are cherished now. We lived in simpler times, and she revelled in them. Pure and proper – and robbed.

Today, I think we also forget too quickly. We move on at speed because the next disaster is just around the corner and the media is lurking there to report it every minute of the day. Then, we had the media for sure, but there was less of it and it was a morning edition in print and a couple of later TV bulletins. On that afternoon when all who knew us from afar stood silently to honour Lesley and respect the family and the horror of this tragedy, the price of life was still valued.

The crowds lined the streets up to the Southern Cemetery, some five miles from the church. The centre of Manchester remained filled with well-wishers. There was no media let-up. Even as we entered the grounds, there was still a TV presence. The police escorted us all the way. Graveyards are horribly silent places at the best of times. There are no best of times. If you think of the coldness, the shiver down your spine when you visit, and find yourself talking to the marble and the slabs of stone and that is bad enough, but nothing compares to that car journey through its grounds at the moment you part with a body.

There is nothing to relieve the moment. A gorgeous autumn sunset or a light-hearted endearing moment between animals can't break the mood. If you saw something funny on the journey into the grounds, your sense of humour is so long departed that you see no bright light on the horizon. There is no respite. Nothing can rescue you from these depths. There is no mood-changer. The silence of the cemetery, accentuated by the turgid speed of the hearse, tear you apart one more time. You don't crave speed and noise, but voids of silence and time are so, so painful, waiting for protocol and ceremony to play out. This is your funeral. This is Lesley's day, but yet the curious nature of any funeral is that it is so choreographed. You are led by strangers in their professional guise who do this for a living, who therefore are conditioned to be without emotion, and manoeuvre you to the next prop or stage of the day. That is not to say they are heartless, but they orchestrate,

82

regardless of where you are up to. After you, there will be another procession and another burial. On a schedule. You are a cog. There is no element of a Lesley's day that is ours. It is a day for everybody else. All the days that follow are ours.

As you pass the hundreds of tombstones – names and families of eras long before you, many who lived a good long life, merged in with those who were also taken too early, there are none…there is nobody who can lay next to Lesley in tragedy. Death is natural, and nothing brings it home more than that drive into the cemetery, even for me at that age. But then nothing underlines the injustice, the blind daylight robbery of it all, and the sheer random cruelty of the circumstances in which we find ourselves here than the stillness of the graves and the dates that reflect their time on earth. Lesley has barely notched a decade. You stare at people whose worlds you will never collide with. Those whom have been here before you, but not under these circumstances, but knowing too that when they made this journey in the hearse, they also felt the ultimate pain.

Unbelievably, there were still many well-wishers – and voyeurs – lingering near the graveside. The police had to erect a cordon around Lesley's final resting place. I am not sure even now why these people felt the need to go the final mile and what possessed them that they had to get so close to the grave. In time, this point of burial would cause us even more pain. In the moment, we just wanted peace and privacy and even if there were nobody but a police escort that is a police escort too many, given what we have been through.

I grabbed Mum closely. We were both so cold and tired. This day had lasted forever. Again, I was a child caught in an adult world, craving a mother, yet parenting my mother, as I pointed out the roses at the head of the grave that we had provided. Mum had barely noticed them in amongst the endless floral display, but also in amongst the blurred vision that grief brought. She was on autopilot, but worse. Transfixed as the description suggests, but so groggy and lost that any conversation was merely a prompt as in 'you need to stand here now, Mum'. None of us were functioning at all. Alan just about held it together. Mum was resorting to basic facial expressions – a nod covering her entire spectrum of emotions.

But even the professionals were struggling. As the Reverend began the Lord's Prayer, his voice faltered too. He must have seen this occasion thousands of times before, but this situation he would never see again.

As his prayer ended, Lesley's coffin was gently lowered. I could barely look, clinging to Mum. It would have been too much for the boys for sure. We just stood there, staring, as the earth was scattered and Our Les disappeared forever into the ground – a dignity only marginally better than the circumstances that befell her. I watched in soul-destroying pain as Alan ushered Mum to throw some soil onto the coffin with a thud that resonated into the silent surroundings. It was symbolic, but I don't know why. It just resonated pain to me. That pain was mental and physical. Mum was close to collapse and had to be helped back to the car.

And therein lies some sort of understanding to the outsider. My mother, besieged by medicine to bring her to this moment, was on the day undone by mental torture that no volume of narcotics could quash. She was corrupted by a mental pain that manifested itself into physical discomfort. That is depression, that is anxiety and that is post-traumatic stress disorder. Essentially, her body was good, but the pain in her mind destroyed her physically as well. That is the illness. When the mind corrupts the body. The thud of the soil hitting the coffin was – as they say – the final nail in the ...coffin.

We turned to leave. Aimless in direction. Reverend Ford helped Mum to the car. We didn't notice at first that Alan had stayed to linger at the side of the grave. Nor did we see the media who had the lot on film, but did at least in the final moment keep their distance, even though we would appear in everyone's lives the next day. There were no other stories.

We lingered waiting for Alan and for the best part of an hour once the lowering of Lesley's coffin had passed, Mum then received well-wishers at the car. They felt the timing was right. We were devoid of clock, exhausted by the ticking of time that accelerated and stood still in equal measures. It is true that the terrible moment at which Lesley's coffin is lowered does draw a line, it is only in that there is no return. For the kind people who had stayed the course, whom I had earlier considered were perhaps outstaying their welcome, they considered this their moment that the line in the sand had been drawn and they could approach the family.

I sat there, wanting it over. Mum, in her grief, retained politeness and found comfort too. Driving away from that cemetery was a point of no return; lingering with people whom we knew and had no knowledge of in equal measure delayed that process, and anything that put off the inevitable was comforting.

For me, they were adult words I did not understand – the same lines over and over again, uttered with total heartfelt compassion and sincerity, but to a young adult as myself – reduced back to a child as I yo-yoed between the severity of the moment and whom I really was, a young man elevated into this story, but a child still craving his mother. As I reflect, I know many of these people did not know Mum or us. A collective grief, I now understand, brings a greater outpouring. In the years since, I have seen it many times since. In 1997 when Princess Diana was killed, the national outpouring was at times greater than for somebody they actually knew. Yes – they felt a connection with her and the tragic events leading up to her death, but they shed tears for a woman they did not know.

And way before that the same happened. I did not evaluate it at the time, but over the years, I came to understand it. Lesley – even to those whose lives she never touched – resonated. She represented something – whatever that was – from youth to injustice, to the random nature of life and death, I do not know.

By the time we got home, via side roads, on advice because of the press, I was clinging to Mum and, despite the huge numbers of people back home, I felt lost in my own surroundings. I was done. Exhausted. I just wanted my Mum.

The throng of people helped. Nobody wanted to go home to an empty house. Not when you found a full one, you just wanted everyone to leave.

Solidarity and solitude – both craved in equal amounts.

But I had nobody. My brothers were rightly gone for the day, and I had to support Mum and yet, nobody seemed to be giving me it back.

People stayed for a polite hour – we needed them there and wanted them gone. Mum and Alan collapsed on the sofa the moment the house was empty. The news was on and I am sure it was all us. I simply do not remember. It was once again noise in the background – Mum, now heavily sedated with pills and me up way beyond my bedtime. I know we all dreamt of Lesley that night. It was the worst of all nights.

To those who say closure, I repeat that there is no such thing. Parking it, yes. And there is an end in that the ceremony draws a boundary and that line in the sand focusses all your emotion in the moment, but it defies the finite nature of the word. Naïve are those who suggest so. To the hangers-on, the well-wishers, to the close family, the local residents who sold and bought the newspapers that told Lesley's 'story', it is the end of the line. They get this closure in that they have done their bit and they now have to move on and get on with their lives, but for those who are left behind – us – they are entering *Groundhog Day* syndrome. Each day the same, and always trance like. Something gives, in time, that makes it a little better and momentarily breaks the cycle. But that is a long way off and you need lots of those little moments before you come close years later to almost unburdening your shoulders of the guilt and the depression that are both self-inflicted and also random cards in the hands of the devil's dealer.

Yet your shoulders always remain sunken, your body language clearly in regression, unable to express the fullest of emotions even when on a high. It shrinks you. It holds you back. Your shoulders only exist to look back warily over them.

Your voice remains muted for years at a time. Laughter comes with guilt. Fresh sadness rarely alters your state of mind because that grimness has never left you. Moments of happiness come with overdoses of reserve. Picking up the pieces means holding back in every aspect of life. I was beginning the process of surviving life. Living it to the full was a challenge too far. I couldn't accept the understanding that from now on my moral responsibility was to live two lives for the one that I assisted in having had taken away from us. My own demons had begun. The reality is that, even at that age, overnight I had become half the person I was.

Chapter 14

Numbness prevailed. The press lingered for a few days, but the following morning there was a stillness in the house that was not becalming or riddled with the customary anxiety. That deathly quiet, in every sense of the word, was the new norm.

It wasn't that there were eggshells to be walked on because of Mum's state. There was just a transfixed glaze of a family alive, but not living – going through the motions and only just about functioning because society had a structure in place, which for the foreseeable future was the only magnetic pull towards the status quo. The world was still revolving. We couldn't get off.

For me, that meant I continued my job at the butcher's. My own money in my pocket was good, but being forced into interaction with colleagues and customers six days a week somehow half took my mind off what I felt I had done. But there was no permanent state of mind – a cut of meat here, a bit of a laugh there and when the chuckles finished, those dark thoughts would come back into my head.

I had at least made a start to get on with life, but there is no escaping from the cruelty of depression that bulldozes uninvited thoughts randomly into your consciousness. That devil of the mind works to no clock either. You can be experiencing better moments, enjoying the company of those who you work with, radiating pride that you are learning a trade and earning a crust – and seemingly forgetting the past, as much as you always want to remember Lesley – and then it comes again. The feeling never leaves you – its ability to infiltrate any moments of tranquillity – almost predictable in its unpredictability.

And in the real world, none of this was going away any time soon. The approach to Christmas 1965 – a time of year that was always now pre-determined to be hell, was dominated by one key event. Ian Brady and Myra Hindley went before a judge in Hyde, Greater Manchester for the first time.

Details were beginning to emerge as to who these characters were. I took very little of it in at the time, but have since pieced together the story in my adult life through press cuttings, Mum's anecdotal recollection, latterly the internet and of course, through the hours of TV programmes that I have seen or at least seen trailed over the years. At times, you wanted to know detail; at others the quest for information had to stop somewhere. The problem is that even today as I write in 2018, people are still making documentaries about the case that won't go away. And yet, you still learned stuff even now. It is a reasonable assumption to make in this case that, for those whose stories we know, there remain untold ones – from lucky escapes to family members. You do not get to adult life without coming into contact with many different types of people, and even though Brady was a loner, his own existence must have cast its spell over people who have never spoken and crave disassociation.

I learnt that Ian Brady was actually Ian Duncan Stewart, born out of wedlock in 1938 to a waitress from a tearoom in Glasgow. His father is believed to have been a reporter and died before his birth. His mother struggled and, before Brady was but one year old, had given him up to the Sloan family, who already had their own children. Brady became Ian Sloan.

His childhood has often been explored, citing this upbringing as the root of the evil. Little is known of the Sloan family, but Heavens only knows what in time they too must have felt. The dye seemingly was cast.

Three significant points seem to lead the way. From Scotland, he took a 'love' of the outdoors. Unconfirmed references suggest he tortured animals. And, he was in trouble at school.

Reading this back, I do not need to know any more. There are enough clues there.

If you have got reeled in over the years to one of these documentaries, or followed the scent of this story, you will not be surprised to learn that from this confused start to life, emerged someone of supreme intelligence. Do criminals and killers fall into two categories – thick idiots or cunning manipulators? We are dealing with the latter here.

He attended Shawlands Academy in Scotland. This was for above-average students, but his behaviour worsened and, before he reached the age I was at the time of Lesley's abduction, he was already a regular before juvenile courts and had abandoned his education, finding work as a tea boy at a shipyard and, worryingly for its parallels to myself and for the metaphorical symbolism of what he became, a messenger at a butcher's.

As you advance through life, these are just details that are a sequence of events. As you look back, you see the path as the butcher in him began to emerge, threatening his first serious girlfriend with a flick knife, resulting in nine charges against him and a condition of his probation that he lived with his own mother.

And that is the key geographical twist that brought him to our doorstep. Crucially too, his Mum had married an Irish man called Patrick Brady.

Ian Stewart was no longer Ian Sloan or living in Scotland.

He had become Ian Brady.

I can only second-guess if this move to Manchester and a new identity finally set Brady loose when the beginnings of evil seem already there. He had a new location and a different identity, but the person within remained – and was getting worse. Being free from the confines of someone else's family and education in the city he grew up in appears historically to be the moment when the character flipped.

Within months of his new job at Smithfield Market in Manchester, he was sent to Strangeways prison for three months. I am sure his juvenile record did not help, but smuggling a sack of lead seals was just the beginning. Still under 18, he was dismissed to borstal for two years and moved around the country until November 1957 when he was released, emerging back in Manchester, struggling to keep down various jobs.

He was reading a lot of Nazi literature and had acquired a motorbike. His preferred destination was the Pennines. He began to study alone in his bedroom and managed to retain employment finally with a chemical company in a suburb of Manchester called Gorton.

Myra Hindley grew up in Gorton.

She was four and a half years younger and suffered a violent childhood at the hands of her alcoholic father and after the birth of her sister, Maureen, was sent to live with her grandmother. Yet, the paternal influence in her was not to be underestimated. Her Dad had been a tough military man and fought extensively in the Second World War, installing that sense of survival and 'defend yourself at all costs' mentality in his daughter. By her own admission, at the age of eight she was street-fighting and hunting down those who challenged her.

One other significant moment in her upbringing seems to have cast that shadow of evil, borne out of revenge. She declined to go swimming one summer day at a disused reservoir. Her friend Michael Higgins drowned in her absence.

From here she turned to Catholicism – and also began bleaching her hair. She was looking for answers, yet rebelling against the tragedy of loss. From blonde, her hair became pink. She got engaged and ended it at 17 and then took judo lessons where her grip on partners was later described as threatening. She too had been fired from her job – for not showing up.

And this is where their paths cross.

Hindley joined Milwards where Brady was working. She took a job as a typist.

At home she was doing her own writing, compiling a diary, detailing her obsession with him, even before she had even spoken to him and while she continued to date other men. By Christmas 1961, they had begun 'dating' with their first night out at a movie called *The King of Kings,* a violent film about the crucifixion.

She knew of Brady's criminal past, but was not swayed and they began a penchant for X-rated cinema, wine and shared reading of Nazi material, often at work and out loud during lunch breaks, with Hindley perfecting the stereotypical Nazi look in *her* appearance, then constantly changing it to become more and more risqué, presumably at his request or in a bid to excite him. She also told a friend that Brady had drugged her.

They submerged themselves in literature, largely of the same genres – philosophy and torture, and joined Cheadle Rifle Club, purchasing guns and splashing out on photographic kit to record their sick fantasies, mostly of each other.

Two years after they met, in the summer of 1963, they began to plot. They were now living together at Hindley's grandmother's house.

Her sister Maureen was seeing a local lad named David Smith. He too, like Brady, had juvenile criminal convictions. They married in August 1964 with Maureen seven months pregnant. As I later learned, you can not underestimate the role Smith played. I also discovered in time that you can not be entirely sure of his account of that role.

The day after the Smith-Hindley wedding, Brady took the four of them to Windermere in the Lake District for the day. Brady and Smith had barely met before this point, but it was here that they fell under each other's spell.

Re-housed in 1964, geographical fate meant that Hindley and Brady were now on our patch. With her grandmother, they moved to Wardle Brook Avenue where they befriended an eleven-year-old girl on the estate, taking her on several occasions to Saddleworth Moor, but without consequence – the likely explanation for her safe return being her proximity to their house. They were, after all, intent on committing the perfect crime and that would include getting away with it. Patricia Hodges was possibly an experiment, almost a dummy run, without anything sinister happening to her, but they had put down their marker in plain sight, but for nobody to see. Patricia Hodges ultimately made way for Lesley – and others.

It was only at trial that the full extent of their crimes – and equally as revolting – their methods, calculation and planning emerged. Just as heart-breaking was the consequence of the web of destruction in that we were soon to learn how our story overlapped with several other grief-stricken families, though astonishingly not all of that would come out until later years, and even to this day, I am not sure that we can be certain of the final number of their victims.

The scene was set. Very soon, the public would hear for the first time, details known only really to ourselves – such as the tape of Lesley, and in turn we would begin the mental scarring of sharing as we cross-referenced grim details with strangers, for whom we would now forever be united in the form of the other victims' families.

The location was Chester Assizes Court. The date was 19 April 1966. The eyes of the world were watching.

Chapter 15

And the world had never seen anything like it. Chester now found itself in the glare of the spotlight. The front pages of its local paper were reporting record crowds at the zoo, despite the weather, together with the news that the Queen was coming to Chester Races. This was simply about to blow everything else away.

The *Chester Chronicle* dubbed it 'The Bodies on the Moors Trial'. The phrase the 'Moors Murders' has become standard in the years since. At the time those words, I believe, reflect the level of mystery and the lack of detail in the public domain pre-trial. The police were in no doubt of what was to come. For the first time in British legal history, the dock was shielded with bulletproof glass, vindicated by the arrest of three people trying to enter the building carrying a gun. Force leave was once again cancelled and officers were drafted in from neighbour counties.

There was also a huge level of fantasy at play. The actor John Mills attended with his wife. One couple from Huddersfield left at 3 am for their big day out, telling the paper that they could not keep away from the trial. Hotels were rammed. Over 150 reporters had descended on Chester. They had already dubbed Hindley 'the most evil woman in the country'. I assume there were no other candidates.

The level of planning even included £2500 worth of public address system and specially installed one-way glass in the police van carrying Brady and Hindley, so the public could not see them.

Mum didn't manage to go every day. I saw her leave and come home in various stages of the emotional cycle. Anger, repulsion, sadness – there were so many ways to get upset and a different detail on a different day would trigger a new reaction. The grieving for Lesley would never end, but the public airing and the representation of the story through legal argument bore a different weight. Heavily medicated, grieving under post-traumatic stress within your own four walls was sheer pain. The unravelling of the story at trial added anger. It almost moved the hurt along a stage. Numbness was replaced by fight. Soft sobbing or hysterical wailing that I had witnessed since that Boxing Day became aggression and disgust. The pain was still there, but the trial was the beginning of the fightback which gave Mum the energy to never let this lie, and in time, take it to the highest platforms in the country.

Make no mistake though, renewed vigour was still exhausting. Stomach-churning anticipation of the day ahead in court was often as draining as the detail. Getting yourself ready and to the court meant you had already had three hours of stress before it had even begun and, when you got there, the media spotlight and the huge crowds just accentuated the point. Uncle Gerald would drive a decoy car ahead as two officers would motion to open the door, while Mum and Alan would pull up with the spotlight elsewhere.

And this would go on and off for 14 days.

It felt like an eternity. Mum was exhausted as you would expect. Two weeks lasted a lifetime. History records it as a fortnight, but when you are in the moment these are just successive days in court. Nobody knows when it will end or how long the jury will need. You once again lose sense of time. You just keep turning up with no end in sight and then it is over. If I had my time again, I do not think I would turn back the clock and attend. For Mum this was more 'closure' than the funeral, but we are dealing in small margins. To get as close as possible to feel like you were looking them in the eye was more than symbolic. It required nerves of steel and a fearless personality – and that was Mum at her best. It is difficult to understand or explain why setting eyes on those two was as close as you can come to a healing moment, revenge, justice – whatever you want to call it, but perhaps it is explained with the knowledge that so much of what lies in the head of these serial killers revolves around the mind and control issues, and this was our only chance to wrestle that back and place level the scales of injustice. Indeed, this was clearly more important than any verdict. Without disrespecting legal process, there could only be one verdict, but there would never be another opportunity to get this close to them.

So, in front of Justice Fenton Atkinson, Brady and Hindley faced charges of three counts of murder – for Edward Evans, John Kilbride and Lesley.

Astonishingly, they both pleaded not guilty. I don't know if that was self-delusion or after legal advice. Brady was being represented by Emlyn Hooson – a Liberal MP. How you would be expected to court the public vote after a trial like this was beyond me.

Both Brady and Hindley were called to give evidence – totalling nearly 15 hours combined testimony. They couldn't have foreseen the defence's star witness though, who gave evidence for a day and a half, but then watched the verdict from home on television – that was the role played by David Smith, a man knee-deep in the Brady-Hindley world, but also exposed mid-trial for entering into an agreement with a newspaper who would buy his story on their conviction and were already keeping him on a retainer, funding him a holiday abroad and putting him up five-star during the trial. Family loyalties were laid bare. He was in on it all, but sold them down the river for his own gain – a crook from start to finish and with loyalty only to himself. The judge described him as having undertaken 'gross interference with the course of justice' but it was clear that with or without Smith's evidence or lack of moral code, justice would reach that end course.

And soon the details emerged of – at this stage – an incomplete picture. There must have been parents absorbing the detail of this trial who had missing children who could only wonder. Brady and Hindley faced only three counts. The truth was somewhat different:

On 12 July 1963, sixteen-year-old Pauline Reade had been their first victim. Brady had told Hindley that night that he wanted to commit the perfect murder. That was the level of pre-meditation. Pauline had been to school with Maureen Hindley and had also had a brief relationship with Smith.

There were no witnesses to Pauline's movements before her death even though she had been on the way to a dance. Hindley had been driving, with Brady behind on his motorcycle when they lured Pauline with ease into the back of the car under the pretence of looking for a lost glove. Pauline, knowing Hindley, innocently agreed.

Once at the moors, Brady cut her throat in Hindley's absence. She stayed in the vehicle, only for her to return to discover Pauline's clothes and leading to the assumption that Brady had assaulted her. They buried the body with a spade Brady had already planted on the Moors, and then drove back into town passing Pauline's Mum and brother en route. Cold-blooded, pre-meditated, and almost mocking cynicism.

On 23 November 1963, poor John Kilbride met his death. This time there had been a colossal search, missing posters and hundreds of witness statements with over 2000 people combing wasteland eight days on, after there had been no sign of John. There was considerable time between the first two murders and the level of response had clearly escalated by November,

but it was still over a week on before it engulfed the community. Hindsight shows you that their crimes were increasing and at this point unstoppable. It makes the delays that night at the police station when Lesley went missing even sadder. To my knowledge, nobody was making any connection at the time between the murders.

In the interim, Hindley had hired several vehicles to visit the burial sites to check that they had not been disturbed. Finding nothing, may have encouraged them that time had passed and they could kill again. I also now understand that this is part of the process undertaken by serial killers – the quest for a 'trophy' or to revisit the scene. From the outside it reads as though Brady was getting Hindley do his dirty work. All of it of course was beyond belief, but she hired the cars, largely flagged down the victims, was often out of sight at the moment of impact, or indeed claimed to be, and then she would have to report back.

Over the years, I have of course had to cross the Pennines many times. Whether it is 1975 or 2015, it sends a chill down my spine. Eerie at the best of time, the highest motorway in Britain looks down across that wasteland into a vast expanse of nothing. Every motorist knows that house in the middle of the motorway and that, for a moment, captures their attention, but if leaving the area, heading north at the point three lanes merge into two, you can see for miles and you can see nothing.

Beyond the volume of traffic over the years, the landscape has barely changed. Other than a chance discovery or a tip off, Brady must have known that he was sending Hindley up there to confirm the graves were undisturbed, rather than check whether they had been. Finding everything as they left it means we are where we are today, in that Winnie Johnson has no grave for her son and that type of barren abandoned landscape would have only given them the green light to proceed. And sadly, Winnie's son was next in the sequence, though this was not known at the time.

On 16 June 1964 twelve-year-old Keith Bennett went missing on his way home to Longsight, Manchester, with his stepfather accused on numerous occasions and their floorboards ripped up in search of a body. Hindley lured Keith into the car. Again, they were looking for a lost glove. Once more Brady had hidden a spade. He sexually assaulted Keith and then strangled him with string.

So, in court next in the sequence came Lesley, as a stunned jury endured the recording with the voices of Brady and Hindley audible – the latter confessing that she had been 'brusque and cruel', but only because she feared someone may hear Lesley screaming. When Lesley was being undressed, she was downstairs. When the pornographic photos were taken, she was looking out the window. On Lesley's strangulation, she was running a bath. An incredible set of coincidences, inaction and lack of remorse. This, I think, is where the anger begins to rise. Mum knew the crimes and the detail concerning Lesley, but she had not seen or heard that attitude and the tone.

The specifics are tough enough to deal with, but when you hear the voice of those telling their version of events and you witness the mindset and the lack of ability to reflect or admit any wrongdoing, then that is when the grief transforms into rage. That lack of reflection though was constant. They were not remorseful because of course, they would move on.

They waited some time before they would strike again. It was 6 October 1965 when Brady randomly selected Edward Evans at Manchester Central Railway Station.

Brady acknowledged that he had hit Edward Evans over the head with an axe, but did not admit killing him, clinging to the small grain in the process that the pathologist's report offered by saying that his death was accelerated by strangulation.

Without a care in the world, Brady concluded that 'if he died from axe blows, I killed him' as though the matter was in doubt and subject to personal interpretation. Meanwhile Hindley denied that the photos of Saddleworth Moor were taken near the graves of their victims.

But Edward's death was the key moment in forming our collective grief, combining our stories and the path to understand the sequence of events, as it was Smith himself who had blown the whistle the previous autumn. There was no mistaking Smith was at the scene as he called the police. The doubts remain as to whether this was his only involvement. Did he just happen to be at the house where Edward had been bludgeoned to death or had he been at others and this was the moment that he had to split ranks?

It seemed unlikely that this was his sole involvement. There were more than two adult voices on the tape of Lesley. I don't think it is unreasonable to conclude that Hindley and Brady's circle extended no further than themselves and Smith and Maureen Hindley, at the very least in terms of awareness, if not participation. Therefore, you would probably suggest that they were both there too. It may be co-incidence, good fortune or plain fact, but the only insinuation of this previously had come from the clairvoyant, who had mentioned four individuals, a motorcycle and a car. The vehicles ring true and now so did the number of accomplices.

Smith clearly had seen a chance to save his own skin. I suspect it would be easy to argue in defence that Brady was a controlling person and before you knew it, you were cast under his spell. If there was grey area with his involvement in the other abductions, there was no denying he was present and complicit at Edwards Evans' death. He chose that moment to cut and run.

In any other circumstances, given his previous convictions and his allegiance to deal-making with the press, he would have been cast as an unreliable witness. The crimes though were so gruesome that only the plea of 'not guilty' from Hindley and Brady stood in the way of a certain conviction.

I shudder at the thought of all of this.

Crucially, as would only become apparent later, Mum and Alan missed his testimony. But their paths were about to cross.

Chapter 16

On 6 May 1966, the jury took just two hours to deliberate. It was that straightforward. Ian Brady was found guilty of all three murders. Hindley was sentenced for Lesley and Edward Evans' killings and, in the case of John Kilbride, for harbouring Brady in the knowledge that he had murdered John. There remains one key detail in their punishment.

Just eleven days before they were charged, the previous autumn, the death penalty had been abolished. It received royal assent on 8 November 1965, coming into effect the next day. Lesley had been discovered on 16 October and John five days later. They were already being held for Edward's murder and, when John was discovered, Brady and Hindley had been brought before Hyde Magistrates Court that same day. They had been taken in separately and remanded in custody for a week. On 28 October, they had made only a two-minute appearance and were detained for a further week. At this stage, Brady only admitted to taking pictures of Lesley, but was adamant that she had been brought to Wardle Brook Avenue by two men who had taken her away alive. One of these could have been Smith or neither may have existed. By 2 December, the new law was in place and four days later, Brady and Hindley were formally charged. In front of three magistrates over eleven days, they were then committed for trial.

There could not have been a more poignant moment for the bill to go through. In Northern Ireland, the death penalty survived until 1973. In Great Britain, it was replaced by life imprisonment. In time, of course, people would come to question if life meant life. Frustratingly, the introduction of the bill was staggered so that it contained a clause which stated that the Act would expire in July 1970 unless Parliament determined otherwise – which it did in 1969, leaving four get-out clauses that included high treason, piracy with violence, arson in royal dockyards, espionage and some capital offences under military law. In some form, the death penalty did survive until 1998, but there have been no public executions since 1964.

Over 200 years of criminal history changed at the time at which two of its most notorious antagonists made the case for it strong. Brady and Hindley would surely have hung. The arguments 'for' are overwhelming – especially when you realise how much their life inside and continued existence added to the pain for the families. I have only really begun to address half a century's worth of grief with Brady's death in 2017.

The arguments 'against' normally centre around making people pay for every day left on this planet, but history will show that it merely allowed Brady, in particular, the opportunity to have a voice, play legal argument and torment the minds of those families whose lives he had ruined. To give you some context, by the 1700s 222 crimes were punishable by death in Britain. They included stealing, cutting down a tree and robbing a rabbit warren. By 1837, the list was reduced to around 100 crimes.

In short, the old Act could punish you for putting your hand in a hole for bunnies. The new one could send you to your death for spying or setting fire to only a royal dockyard. These broadest of parameters left no space for the termination of Myra Hindley and Ian Brady.

So, Brady received three concurrent life sentences and Hindley two plus seven years for 'harbouring' Brady. They were instantly separated. Brady was sent to Durham and Hindley to Holloway, the all women and young offenders' prison in London.

The judge's closing remarks described the murders as a 'truly horrible case', citing Brady and Hindley as 'two sadistic killers of the utmost depravity', with the former 'wicked beyond belief' and recommended that they spend a very long time in prison. He doubted that Brady in particular could reform, though inferred that, free from him, Hindley perhaps could. There was the carrot, at which she began to nibble almost instantly. At this stage neither showed any level of regret, relentlessly lying at every stage. Even in 1965, there were now doubts that life meant life.

The legislation, of course was being prepared irrespective of their arrest, but there is probably no greater case in British legal history where the moral fibre of an Act being passed was so instantly tested. And this now is where the story begins to take a new shape because the fall out from these crimes meant that at every turn, there was a knock-on effect.

At the General Election of March 1966, there was a surprising name on the ballot paper for the constituents of Nelson and Colne in Northern Lancashire. My Dad's brother decided to run on a one ticket candidacy. I am not sure he got as far as having any real policies if he were elected, but in the immediate aftermath of the Act *but* before the details of the trial which followed within the next month, he decided to test the electorate's mettle on the issue. Nothing could have propelled a single issue more into the spotlight at election time, unless the vote had come after the trial, at which point the true extent of the detail would have been known. Amidst great publicity, he won 51,117 votes, amounting to nearly 14% of the total. As is often the way when a one-horse candidate runs, the individual may not succeed, but did manage to re-energise the hanging issue amongst the Conservatives, with one former cabinet minister trying to launch a bill by that autumn to reverse it, notably for the crime of killing police officers.

It is impossible to speculate on the public's mood and my own stance on the issue is obviously clouded. Outside of my own life, if none of this had happened, what would I think? I can't know. Nor can anyone gauge the level of success that Uncle Pat might have had if it had been post-trial? A huge argument for pro-hanging has always been a life for a life. Brady and Hindley took at least five.

One man remained free – and that was David Smith. He was free in the literal sense of the word, but his freedom was severely tarnished. It is not even a difficult one to call for most people and I think now *he* had miscalled his own hand. Whether he had options, once he had entered Brady's world it was a moot point – but he did have a criminal past too. Little scorn is poured upon Maureen Hindley, so that would suggest that he was in too deep and misjudged how his own actions would be perceived.

So, despite bringing Brady and Hindley down, there was a backlash. Maureen Hindley was attacked during the trial, eight months pregnant at the time. Their home and the lift to it were vandalised. Hate mail was regular. Their own children could not play out.

However, some level of consciousness or guilt struck David Smith. In 1966, not long after sentencing, the most extraordinary event occurred. I was sat on the stairs one day at the house in Hattersley when there was a thunderous knock at the door. Originally, people didn't know who we were, but it never took long. As we were about to discover.

Mum was resting and heavily medicated, so Alan went to answer.

'Do you know who I am?' he asked.

Alan didn't. So, he announced himself, standing there in his black coat and dark glasses.

'My name is Dave Smith.'

Alan was still clueless. There had been so many knocks at the door – so many strangers, family and friends, officers, undertakers, press. Though it had begun to subside, it was just another intruder.

Then he uttered the words that made us stop in our tracks.

'I'm Hindley's brother-in-law. I gave evidence against them at the trial.'

His language was deliberate to position himself at distance from them, even though he still lived with a Hindley.

Still, Mum did not stir. But Alan let him in, commenting after that Smith was very nervous. I remember following them into the living room and hearing words nobody will ever forget.

'Isn't he like Lesley?'

104

That woke Mum up. I was none the wiser, not really understanding the significance of the man or the words.

Ask anybody though who has been in situations deemed similar to ours and they will tell you that amongst all the brutal facts, the uncertainties sap you of the energy life requires and prevent you moving on, and often the chief characteristic is a turn of phrase that doesn't seem to fit. It plays over in your mind for years and you never get an explanation.

Smith's hesitant nature subsided slightly once in the house. He must have spent the journey there wondering if he would get through the door. Once he had been let in, his guard slipped. He knew exactly who I was and from his subconscious he made the immediate parallel.

At the time, I was not sufficiently on the ball or old enough to realise what he was saying, but my goodness, I have had plenty of opportunity since. It leaves me in no doubt that he had spent almost as much time with Lesley as Brady and Hindley – that nagging feeling that he had more than Edward Evans' blood on his hands, the clairvoyant citing four individuals, the voices on the tape, Brady suggesting that two other people were involved…where in all this was the truth? That was more than a slip of the tongue. It came with knowledge. It also implied post-involvement in that way that killers like trophies and to revisit the scene, they like to study what is written about them and, at times, can be compulsive obsessives. Yes, there were pictures of me in the public domain, notably the funeral, but none were recent. Nor was he introduced to me. It felt like he had been building up to this visit and had absorbed as much as he could about the family and the case. Relieved at being allowed in, he just blurted it out.

Mum now feigned sleep – it seems the slumber of medication can be interrupted when the moment merits it.

He was pleading his case, making a pitch to be the good guy. Yet, one thing rang true. Parts of what he said were inconsistent with what the police had told us and, more

105

importantly, what had been heard in the court of law. He described Edward's death in a brutal narrative, but also in bizarre obscure detail, which included Myra Hindley summoning him to bring a pram round their house – something he failed to do. Inside he found Hindley semi-naked and offering herself up for Edward, with Brady standing behind with the axe.

Smith maintains that Myra Hindley described the scene as 'the messiest one yet' – a phrase which underlines their quest, sick pleasure, and lack of remorse. Then he told stories of days out with Brady, from his disgusting sense of humour to terrorising motorists. It was all vile, but somehow at its heart lay self-justification. Alan eventually had to usher him out of the property, but his presence had left a devastating effect.

Mum questioned too that he must have some role in Lesley's abduction – again, Brady and Hindley or two people bringing Lesley to the house and taking her away. Then, those words. They resonated deeply. Didn't I look like Lesley?

We knew little of this individual, other than that he was chief witness and married to Hindley's sister. We soon discovered that his childhood was similar to Brady's, in that his mother, Joyce Hull, disappeared when he was less than a year old. David Smith had been David Hull. His father, Jack Smith, passed him to his own parents, who adopted him, returning to Gorton at the age of six to live with his Dad and by eleven he had wounded a fellow pupil and was expelled for punching the headmaster on the nose. It didn't get much better at secondary school and, by fifteen, Smith had met Maureen Hindley and had abandoned education. He too was often fired from work. Marrying Maureen Hindley, when discovering she was pregnant, it transpires that the trip to the Lake District the next day was a honeymoon gift from Brady.

Within a few days of him turning up at ours, Mum and Alan were at boiling point and decided to take the matter into their own hands, tracking down Smith to his home. From details that emerged at court, they had a vague sense of where he lived, but so strong was the anti-Smith feeling that locals were happy to point them on their way to his house. Graffiti lined the walls of the estate too saying 'Child Killers Live Here'. Everyone else had made their mind up.

They too were now drawn to communicate with Smith. This was different. Alan knocked twice to no answer. They could see there were lights on inside. Then anger took over. Alan began to kick the door down.

Inside the house, Mum grabbed Maureen Hindley's hair, insistent on taking a photo of her for the family resemblance, should Myra Hindley ever needed tracking down. Mum took to Maureen Hindley and Alan sorted Smith, leaving them both bloodied and spinning. I know it helped Mum and Alan release some tension, and they slept soundly that night. Smith had realistically invited the situation. Mum and Alan were not ever going to go looking for him, but his insistence in offloading and that slip of the tongue condemned him. In a world where our life seemed an injustice, dishing out our own seemed fair.

But then, early the next morning, there was another tap at our door. Two police officers had come to discuss the incident the previous evening. Maureen Hindley had presented a clump of hair as evidence. It seemed extraordinary. Back then, people sorted stuff out like that. They seemed to think they were floating above the law when of course they had fallen well below its radar.

On this occasion there would be no charges against Mum and Alan. If it happened again there might be. I don't think anybody cared. The thought that Smith had called the police lingered. Up to his neck in it, he turned to the law to defend himself against those whom he aggressed in their own home and whose family he had some role in tearing apart. When you had been through everything Mum and Alan had, you just simply didn't care. If Smith and Hindley were above the law, then we were beyond it.

But it simply did not end there. In 1969, Smith was sentenced to three years in prison for stabbing a man in a fight in response to abuse he had received for his role in proceedings. He had regularly been beaten up in pubs. Maureen Hindley then lost custody of her children, who were taken into care, and after Smith's release, the pair divorced. Smith attempted suicide. In 1972, he was acquitted of the murder of his father, who had been suffering from an incurable cancer. Offering a plea of manslaughter, he received just two days detention.

Maureen Hindley died of a brain haemorrhage in 1980. Smith moved to Ireland to run a bed and breakfast with his second wife, succumbing to cancer in 2012 after years of smoking.

A confession from Hindley in 1987 exonerated Smith from his role in the Moors Murders, but can that really mean anything or have any weight when he was at the very least present at Edward Evans's death and Brady, for whatever reason, had already alluded to a role in Lesley's disappearance?

He certainly had his own violent streak and was more than likely engulfed in something bigger than he could have imagined through family ties and early admiration for Brady, but life after court showed that he too was capable of enforcing evil, always ready-made with an excuse.

And still today, I hear those words.

'Doesn't he look like Lesley?'

Me and our Les with Father Christmas, 1957

Me aged 12

Our Tommy, Les and Brett

Our Les and Tommy

Me with our Tommy and Brett

Me and Linda on our wedding day

A selection of letters from Ian Brady and Myra Hindley

2/2/89

Dear Mr West,

Thank you for your letter an
press cuttings you took the trouble to se
Re the "tartan album" — the police appear
using double-talk. Mr Allen Bennett also s
police and they said it was "up to the fam
and he himself added "whatever that mean
Going by the past bungling of the police,
wouldn't be at all surprised to discover th
have lost or sold to the media their copy q
album.

Re your wishing to use extracts of my let
a book. I have no objections, provided
shown in advance the extracts which the a
wishes to publish — I stipulate this to en

being taken against three different nationa
newspapers for breach of copyright becaus
printed extracts of letters I had sent in
confidentiality to someone else.

I am still giving as much assistance a
re other cases, but it is difficult to do
remote control. Mr A. Bennett says that t
police are now most interested in the two
shootings — one in England, the other Sco.

Sincerely,

H. Brady

6/5/88   490, Ian Stewart Brady
                Park Lane Hospital,
                Liverpool.

Dear Mrs West,
                Thank you for your
letter.
      I am not receiving sufficient
medication to relax, so my ability
to ~~con~~ concentrate is hampered.
      I have been reliably informed
that Channel 4 T.V. intends to
screen a play about the case next
month.
                Sincerely,
                      I S Brady

20/6/87   490, I. Brady,
           Park Lane Hospital
           Liverpool.

Dear Mrs Hert,
                Many thanks
for your last letter.
The reason I have not replied
sooner is that many things
that are happening must not
reach the press yet.
    I suppose you've seen or heard
that the Home Office, on the
strength of my information, are
re-opening the case.
I can't tell you anything
else. You'll see or read about
it soon.
            Sincerely,
                Ian Brady

P.T.O.

115

PS: I'm glad you got on well with my mother. She knows nothing at all about the moors, etc.

In replying to this letter, please write on the envelope:
Number 964055 Name HINDLEY

PNFP
©

Monday 28·9·87

Dear Mrs. West,

Thank you for your letter, and I'm sorry it has taken me so long to reply to it. I think I know how difficult it must have been to write to me, and this reply is going to be even more difficult, because I find it almost impossible to express the way I feel about the indescribable suffering I have caused you, your family and the other families concerned.

It is true what you say in your letter about my never having written to you during all these years to express any sorrow or remorse, but I want you to know that in the early 1970s, after having read something about you in the press, I did ask the authorities in Holloway if I could write to you (rules about correspondence have changed in the last few years), and if I could ask you to visit me, despite your threats to kill me if you ever get the chance to. But I was advised against writing, and an adamant refusal was given for a visit to take place.

In retrospect, I know the letter I would have written then would not have been as frank as

No. 243A 34095 14/7/82 XBD

117

this one will be, because you must be aware that it has taken me a very long time – much too long – to come to terms with what Ian Brady and I did all those years ago. I could not even face the truth myself, let alone tell the truth to anyone else. This is unforgivable, and I do not expect anyone, especially yourself, to understand the reasons for my long silence and many denials.

I know almost everyone describes me as "cold and calculating – "evil Myra" – but I ask you to believe that I find all this deeply upsetting. I was evil, and I make no excuses whatsoever for my part in any of the past. The letter from Mrs John last October absolutely devastated me, and made me actually realize that I could no longer remain silent whatever the cost to my family or myself. In February this year I gave as full and detailed account as I could to Mr. Topping of what happened to your daughter. I now want to say to you, and I implore you to believe me, because it is the truth, that your child was not physically tortured, as it widely believed.

I said at my trial, and I say to you now, that my involvement in the events on that tape recording was indefensible and that I accepted any derogatory adjective used to describe my conduct. But please believe me – not for my sake, but simply in the hope that it will give you even a little peace of mind, that however monstrous and unforgivable the crime was, your child was not tortured to death.

I want to take this opportunity to say that there was no "third man" involved in your daughter's case. Ian Brady and I lied at our trial about my former brother-in-law's alleged involvement. If this led you to believe he was implicated, as I recollect was the case, then his liberty over the years may have been a source of distress to you. But he didn't have anything to do with it, and I have done him a worse injustice in this respect than he did me by giving false evidence for the Crown about the death of Edward Evans, when in fact he should have been charged and put in the dock with Ian Brady and myself.

But to return to your letter, you say "I could never blame your mother for what happened. It wouldn't be right. So I don't expect you to blame me for all the heartaches I have had over these years." Of course it wouldn't be right to blame my mother. She, and Mrs Brady, are, in a different sense, two more innocent victims of Ian Brady's and my perpetrations. My own mother, and my family, have endured terrible sufferings through me, and are still serving, like yourself, an unbearable life sentence. This is yet another burden of guilt I carry, and the weight of it is almost

119

more than I can bear. The same is true of the sufferings and heartaches I have caused you and the other families. How can I possibly blame you for the thing I am responsible for? And how can I blame you for the more than understandable hatred you feel for me? I do understand your hatred, of course I do, but believe me Mrs. West you couldn't hate me more than I ~~could~~ hate myself. I have asked God for His forgiveness, but I couldn't ask for yours, for how can I ever expect you to forgive me when I cannot forgive myself. I have to live with the past for the rest of my life, with self-inflicted wounds to my mind and heart which I doubt will ever heal. Having finally and fully acknowledged and confessed those heinous crimes, and realized the dreadful enormity of them, the guilt and remorse I feel is agonizing — the wounds have re-opened again and are raw-edged and festering. But I deserve it all, because irrespective of how I became involved in those monstrous crimes at the age of 20, I was a woman; a young one, but still a woman, and an utter disgrace to womankind, as you yourself have said, as have others, and rightly so.

Mrs West, can I ask you to believe the woman I now am, aged 45, that I am not what I was all those years ago, and to accept that

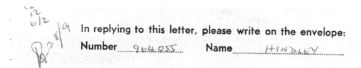
my sincerity is genuine in respect of my
deep regret and remorse for all the pain and
heartache I have caused you and your family.
No words can adequately express what I feel,
or what I wish with all my heart you could
understand. To say 'I'm truly and deeply
sorry' sounds so futile, but I am truly and
deeply sorry, and sorry also for taking all
these years to say so. In the past it
seemed an impossible task to write to you
when you were quite rightly fighting so
hard against my release from prison. There is
no need to do that any longer, because
I have finally accepted my fate, and know
that release from prison is no longer a
practical reality. I have written to the
Home Office and the Parole Board to say I
do not wish to be considered for parole in
1990, and my own belief is that I shall
probably remain in prison until I die. So be
it. I've brought it all on myself.

    Since my confession to Mr Topping
in February this year, the police have been

No. 243A 34095 14/7/82 XBD

121

able to find Pauline Reade's body, and her family have been able to give her a Christian burial at last. I am deeply sorry that the case is not yet true for Keith Bennett. I pray and hope with all my heart that the police resume the search and I promise you, as I am writing to Mrs. Johnson to promise her, that I will continue to do everything possible to help them find her son so that she and her family can be relieved of some of their grief. It is true I wanted to send a message to the Reade family, but I was advised against it, as it was feared it would intensify their grief. But Mass was said here for Pauline and her family, and I will write to them when I feel they are able to accept a letter from me.

There is one last thing I would like to say to you. As I wrote above, I do understand your hatred, and I've said that you couldn't hate me more than I hate myself. I know that nothing can change the past, and that you can never forgive or forget the loss of your child, or that any words of mine can bring her back to you. But what I do wish for you, Mrs West, is that eventually your hatred can subside

to
to enable you gain some measure of peace
of mind. I know from my self-hatred that
it corrodes the spirit and leads to a
despair that is unbearable to live with.
You've suffered more than enough; please
don't add to your suffering by a hatred
that I'm not worthy of, and will fester in
your heart and mind more than it already
has, through my fault.

 This has been a very long letter and
will have been painful for you to have read
just as it has been painful for me to
have written, knowing that it will have
re-opened your own wounds yet again.
I want to say to you from my heart, as
God is my witness, that my sorrow and
remorse for everything is truly genuine, and I
hope that you accept it as the truth.
If you can't bring yourself to believe me —
and I have no ulterior motive in writing to
you other than my genuine wish to answer
your letter — I will try to understand, and
will continue to pray for you, for peace for you,
and a healing of your pain and heartache.

    Yours sincerely,
     Myra Hindley.

7/3/90

Dear Mr West,

Thank you for your letter of
2/3/90.

Despite my informing you in great detail my
reasons for not answering any more questions
piecemeal from individual families, ie, the fact
that my letter to Mr Paul Reade ended up in
the Sun and that he and my solicitor are
taking actions against that newspaper, you
unfortunately fail to understand the situation.

I am well aware that all the families
concerned are being hounded by the gutter
press for any scrap of information they can
sensationalise. I do not intend to give them
any. I want no more media circuses.

Yes, you did tell me what Topping said, but I
also told you what he said; ie, that your wife
was a woman who "thrived on publicity and
kept a video library of all her T.V. appearances".

This is precisely the trivialisation of issues I
am determined to avoid. I must take into
consideration the wishes of all the families

P. T. O

124

concerned, not just one. All the questions of all the families will be answered and published in great detail. The mass of facts and evidence I am now gathering together will leave no doubt as to their authenticity and will end the 25 years of inventions by hack journalists, authors and all other people out to make fast money without regard to the effect their concocted stories have had on the families concerned.

I will relate the full story, not just bits and pieces, for all the families.

Re visits. Your wife already knows that when she asked to visit me both Dr MacCulloch and Topping refused permission and stated that "under no circumstances" would she be allowed into this hospital. If you believe I am misrepresenting the situation, please write direct to the hospital authorities. They know that if your wife were allowed to visit, the news would immediately be leaked to the media by someone and that there would be masses of cameras outside the gate.

I repeat, I am acting on behalf of all the families concerned, not just one.

You appear to be forgetting that Topping is yet to face the two high court writs re his selling Hindley's phoney confessions for a fortune to the Sun. He and the Sun lawyers are playing for time, waiting for the wave of public opinion against them to die down. They will use anything to distract attention from the main issue.

Sincerely, H Brady.

Me and our Chaz on my wedding day to Linda

Our Chaz and Alan

Me and Mam

My Mam with our Tommy

My Mam, Dad (Terry Snr) and Grannie Downey

Once a happy family – Me, with Mam, Tommy, Brett and our
Les, Blackpool, 1963

Christmas get together, 1998, with Lesley, Chaz, Lin, Me, Mark and our Tommy

Me and my rock, Linda

Chapter 17

I had felt a heaviness in the fortnight of the trial. But when I watched it on the news, I felt proud. I am not sure why – whether it was the supreme effort required by Mum and Alan to keep their dignity in a very public showdown, or because so many people turned out for Our Lesley. Perhaps, it was just huge relief that justice had been done, though there was still the feeling that three life sentences still fell short of what was required and a few months earlier the death penalty would have been a done deal. After all, three life sentences that run concurrently in effect only mean one life sentence and spare Brady, in particular a brutal and public end that would in the smallest way possible mirror our loss of Lesley.

We wanted justice and we wanted it over, but that closure line rears its ugly head again. We wanted it over when Lesley was not found, then again when she was. Fast forward to the funeral and people say you can move on, but then there is still the trial and following that, the fall-out with Smith.

So, closure is non-existent. All you are doing is putting distance between you and the moment, but there was and is still always something. And we were a long way away from the end of this story by the summer of 1966.

Indeed, football had been my only real release. I can barely recall that England won the World Cup and there can not be many people of my age whose memories of it are so shot to pieces. It would have been the ideal opportunity to switch off and revel in the one true thing I could lose myself in, but the trance was still there and the glazed look never went away. I had become immune to the highs and lows of life. Extremes ceased to exist, replaced by a treadmill of numb.

Psychologists dub periods like this 'fight or flight' – you either stay and guts it out or you run. I felt that there was little to keep me. I had been robbed of an innocence at the start of my teens and, through no fault of her own, my relationship with Mum took a back seat. She still had time for us, but she was constantly fighting the medication and continual stress of the latest knock at the door or false report in the news. The air that the story was unfinished always lingered. I felt for the way it affected her.

And Christmas 1966 was depression personified. The joy of the day just simply did not exist. The atmosphere was sombre at best. We had set a place for Lesley and would continue to do so, but whether we went through those motions or not, you felt her presence *and* the void she left behind. Guilt extends to many levels – from my own personal remorse at two previous Christmases, to the sheer notion that it was meant to be the happiest day of the year and yet, your emotion remained reined in. You are never quite able to lose yourself in joy. Tommy and Brett were now that little bit older and were starting to really absorb the atmosphere. The trial cast a shadow that, with Christmas, came the knowledge that the next day was Boxing Day, and that meant the fair just underlines that these were now days you had to get past, rather than enjoy, but how long would it be before you stopped seeing an obstacle in every moment in time? Mum had only recently drawn a line under Lesley's untouched bedroom. Though we had moved since that day, it remained a shrine, originally under the self-persuading belief that we were keeping it in the hope that she would return home, but when hope left us, there was never a moment or a day when anyone had said 'maybe it is time to sort Lesley's stuff out.' Then so much time has passed that this too becomes the norm – Lesley's untouched bedroom, and that is where the realities become blurred. No longer holding out hope and not even contemplating that it might be disrespectful to remove her material possessions, there just never was any need. We had waited so long, preserving her place, that by the time her fate was finite, it was just another room in the house. Obviously, you passed her room every day, occasionally putting your head around the door and staring into the space, seeing Lesley before you, but without the physical her being present. On other days, you brush past as though it is a room with a No Entry sign on it. It depended on how you felt in that moment. I think Mum spent a lot of time in there and when it finally came to Alan to find a new home for Lesley's stuff, we were in effect re-arranging the furniture. You would never discard it, just move it along.

And even though Boxing Day loomed as the anniversary, places were set – I am sure – and bedrooms left untouched in the other victims' houses. Please remember that by Christmas 1966, we were 'lucky' in the grim knowledge that we had a body. For those who didn't, I am sure that empty space was left and that bed untouched for even longer, and of course, they were the ones we knew about. The list of phrases that always ran through your mind also included Mum's firm belief:

'There will be more,' she said after Lesley was found, and again after trial.

So, by 1967, perhaps understandably, I chose flight. Not literally, because my method of departure was the opposite, but in the psychological sense. I decided to join the Merchant Navy. My ship set sail for Canada.

I was none the wiser about travel, but I soon learned that Canada was an exciting place to be that year. From the Manchester Liners, we made for Ireland and Belgium. I worked as a steward in the canteen, largely keeping myself to myself, finding it difficult to forge lasting friendships.

When I arrived in Canada, Quebec was hosting Expo '67 – a six-month long world fair of over 60 nations and leaving a general good feeling about the city. Canada was celebrating its centenary. Over 50 million people attended. All round the world it was the summer of love, but I was not really party to that, spending most time at sea. If you asked me why I joined, it was on Mum's recommendation. It really was the press intrusion that led to me to escape. She thought it was best that I attempt to begin afresh and there really was no reason not to. Of course, there were days when the expanse of the ocean was exactly where your thoughts drifted, but equally I found comfort that nobody knew where I was, and for a moment at least, notwithstanding the rules of my employer, I had stepped out of society. When we came ashore, I began a little to find my feet. I didn't entirely let the summer of love pass me by! It remained the calmest period I had experienced in the previous two years and I began to re-connect a little with my emotions. I almost never spoke of what had gone on. Some, I am sure, knew my identity. But I had at least begun to take those baby steps to attempt to forge a life.

One step forward, two back – as they say. It really had been the right thing to do.

I was home on leave when I learned that tragedy had struck the family a second time. Mum had kept it from me while I was away. My Mum's sister, Auntie Elsie and Uncle John had a son – my cousin – called John Forest. He had been admitted to hospital for a routine operation to remove his adenoids, but nobody knew he had some sort of allergy to the anaesthetic. He never woke up and died after surgery. Misfortune was beginning to accumulate. And then there are the details of what he left behind, unbeknownst to him.

John had been courting a girl called Sheila. Sheila had fallen pregnant. A few months later she gave birth to Alex, who is now approaching fifty.

It was not the last time the family would be ripped apart by tragedy and another generation would deal with the consequences.

Chapter 18

I did not return to the Merchant Navy. I had taken giant leaps and whilst there is no league table in death, in that you can't compare Lesley's to my cousin's, obviously the brutality of my sister's murder and at that age still haunted us.

John too, was taken too early and there are simply no parallels, but the collective weight of another death in the family made those shoulders shrink back into depression. Everything just became that bit heavier once more – a swirling of emotions from injustice to the whole business of organising another funeral.

I had returned home assuming that my stay would be brief, but you get pulled back into family drama and there is no right time to leave when grief dominates. So, I just didn't go back.

Time away had given me some clarity and escape, though more so the latter. In reality, nothing was clearer because I didn't discuss it. Any different view on what had happened didn't really exist in my head. I was still guilty and responsible and it remained a series of terrible crimes inflicted on those so young. But 'clarity' did exist in that at least, I had left 'these four walls'. Of course, our life had been constantly on the move as Mum fought housing associations to improve our lot, but essentially we had always lived around the same areas and struggled to survive, and wherever the house was we had felt imprisoned in it since Lesley's death, and constantly under scrutiny outside it. Beyond those four walls I had never really been anywhere.

I don't know how Mum viewed me when I came back. The dark shadow haunted me, but I know I was that little bit more ready for the world. And how did I find Mum?

It is a difficult question. Perhaps my absence had helped *her*. She needed the space and couldn't give me the maternal counselling that I really needed. I think she had felt that if I was forced into such an extremely different environment, other people would move me on. She still had Tommy and Brett to nurture, but they were not carrying the demons of not going to the fair and had the key difference of only understanding events retrospectively. Their pain was in delay.

I still found her heavily medicated and soon understood that this would always be the way. She described life to me as a daily mourning where some days were less bad than others. Life went on, but part of coping was grieving.

By the late 1960s, Terry Downey had become Terry West. Mum asked me to do it and if I was happy to do so. I agreed – anything to protect us from the press intrusion and put a smile on Mum's face. It was a cosmetic change. I think, for her, it was the only way she could separate the eras. Nonetheless, in my heart I always remained a Downey.

But she had something resolute about her. That feisty determination was beginning to return and, in Myra Hindley in particular, she had set her sights. I see now that this is maternal instinct. There is no understanding at this stage as to the mind of Brady, but it remained tougher for Mum to understand how a woman – a relatively new Auntie – could abandon that female gene and do this to another mother and a little girl. She would struggle to spar mentally with Brady and he could be left to rot in her eyes, but she was determined to have it out with Hindley. Behind bars and protected, or the possibility of her freedom, Mum was watching her every move and began the process of attempting to get some control over her. However, many years it would take, she would be watching and grind her down. If you didn't still fight for Lesley until the day you no longer physically could, then your purpose was redundant. Mum made it her mission.

Life remained tough. The family moved to Sale, just a few miles from the centre of Manchester. The practical consequences of what had happened left lasting repercussions. Money had been a constant worry. Now it was a major problem. Alan had missed so much work that work no longer missed him, and he went through a succession of jobs from the Gas Board to driving, to running the ice cream van, but his refusal to take his home life to work and confide in his bosses about what was really going on, cost him dearly and patience was in short supply. Brett was still young and, at times, Mum could barely look after him. Often, he was not seen at work for weeks and there was no aid or government support for families like us. Some two to three years after Lesley's abduction, we still had almost nothing to live off and with no hope of regular attendance at work, let alone being able to concentrate for long periods of time. You can see perhaps why the navy was one of my few options.

We later discovered that in fact there had been compensation available to us, but nobody told us. By the time Mum applied two decades later, she was informed that she should have done so within three years of Lesley's body being discovered. After-care was lacking in those days. It was enough to medicate Mum with drugs, but therapy and practical know-how were thin on the ground. In the time limit on the compensation there also lay the assumption that you would probably be just fine to get on with things after three years, when in reality it damaged an entire lifetime.

Finally, Mum had to resort to her standard method in a bid to get what she wanted, so set off to Derbyshire to the National Assistance Board. This time Brett was the prop after she had been knocked back on countless occasions.

Livid and demanding to know why money was being spent on Brady and Hindley, but not on clothing for my younger brother, she left him on the desk, turned around and walked out. Behind her were the tears of Brett and astonished protests from the staff. Mum made it clear – we can't look after him, so you will have to. She still had her wits about her. That fight was back in small doses. And just as she was about to leave, she was halted at the door and offered a one-off payment of £7. That was it. In today's money, a sum of around £130...so simple to obtain and so paltry in her purse. We would never turn it down, however derisory, but in that moment, it dawned on Mum that we were on our own and that we would forever be fighting authorities on every front. There was one outcome. The campaigner in her was born and would consume her for the rest of her life, however much society put obstacles in her way.

And Brett had replaced me. I had been there on that table once before too and now I was moving on and Brett was learning the way the family operated.

I had previously been unable to over-compensate since Lesley. That 'come on crack a smile' brigade just fell on deaf ears and only accentuated our loss, but the time away had forced me into a situation and a new form of coping, so once I decided I was not going back, I also realised that it was time to move out. Mum had probably got used to the four of them, when once we had been six, and being away had given me that insight into adult life and forced me to cope on my own. I think once you have lived at sea and lived away, coming home is a temporary need for Mum's cooking or your favourite chair, but in reality, you need to start finding your own place. Plus, I had also begun seeing Lorraine, whom I had met at the Pop Inn, a local club near Platt Lane.

Times were different then, for sure. People married younger and quicker and probably stayed together, so in no time at all we were married…by 1970. In effect, a couple of years after I came back from sea, I decided to settle down.

It is difficult to know if I was just doing what everybody was doing around my age, a couple of years into working life. Maybe I was beginning to have a good time, going out to the pubs and finding the confidence to chat to girls – or perhaps I was desperate to climb into a void. The way to move on was to jump straight into adult life. A new family would be the answer and, whilst I would always be part of my own and close to them, if I was going to make anything of my life amidst all this grief, then this was probably the way. A safety net, I think.

I was beginning to make strides, but a long way from releasing the demons that remained. It took me a good few months before I told Lorraine anything about Lesley and who I was. It is a difficult conversation to have. When will the time ever be right to do so? What if this person is not the right one for you and you have blurted it all out, which is something I was never likely to be able to do too many times in life? And even though, it should not affect that other person's opinion of you, as it is a crime that befell your family, what if it was too much for them? Perhaps they knew anyway? Wherever Mum moved us, the press still lurked now and then and there was no hiding from curtain-twitchers and neighbourhood gossips, but I had time and distance in place by going away and moving out and, however hard it was to attempt to move on, surely I deserved that right to try and forge my own identity?

As I hope any reasonable person would do, Lorraine understood and said little, except that she was glad that she had found out from me and nobody else. There was no way that we could make a life together and me not tell her. I realise now that the press could turn up at any point and not realising how the media really worked, the fifth anniversary, the tenth anniversary, a fresh discovery on the Moors, or us driving past to Yorkshire, or Brady or Hindley making news for themselves...any of this could just re-emerge at a random moment. She needed to know and it was unavoidable.

Plus, there was Mum. She was beginning to find her feet and make a lot of noise. While we were starting out on our life together, she was devoting the rest of hers to ensuring justice remained and Lesley's memory would be preserved forever.

I settled into married life and was able to leave a little of the past behind, but there was always something not quite right, which was nobody's fault. So few people (essentially Mum and I) can relate to Lesley's tragic loss, that it just overshadows everything. When people make comments like 'there were three people in this marriage', I could be accused of going the other way. In many ways, Lorraine must have felt it was just *her*. There were so many times when the early giddy times had passed that I was just unable to express myself.

Some conversations would begin with 'What are you thinking…a penny for your thoughts…' and I would just reply 'Oh nothing', but that was clearly just code that my head was being battered with thoughts and responsibility. It did affect our relationship and when Charlene was born relatively quickly into the relationship in June 1971, followed two years later by Alan, the two life moments that perhaps could finally set me free and create my own identity held me back even more, especially with Chaz, because all I saw in her formative years was Lesley. It is no surprise that in fact we named her Charlene Lesley.

It never got any better. If you think of the five-minute walk to the fair that Boxing Day as the yardstick, every measure of a distance was comparable to that. So, I saw fear when Charlene would leave through the garden gate and that became a symbol of me being irresponsible. If she passed that, even though we lived in a cul-de-sac, she had wandered into territory where my eyes could not see her any more. In other words, she had gone to the fair too.

When it came to friends' birthday parties and she could be gone for a few hours, I would attend, and school trips away only happened at High School and were only agreed to with an anxiety-ridden reluctance. If the day came when I would take her to that year's funfair at Wythenshawe Park, I was petrified. Eyes in the back of my head were not enough. I stuck to her like glue and would get in and out as quickly as possible. The Moors had become the big symbol to the public, with its barbaric landscape and the imagery of those so very young being slain and abandoned and buried in the ground in terrain few visited. But for me, Hattersley and the Boxing Day Fair was the image I could not get passed. The problem in my mind was the dislocation of time. I knew that fair inside out. Year after year the same stalls stood in the same place but the one year that I do not go is the moment Lesley is taken and I try to rewind the tape and place myself in that setting, guessing her way round, grabbing at invisible air, trying to clutch her back before evil snatched her for good. There was no way that was going to happen to Charlene.

This possibly meant that Alan was left out. Much of my pre-occupation was with Charlene. Alan, therefore, was quite reticent, but at the other end of the spectrum, could be outspoken if needed to be. I totally understand that dynamic. My over-bearing nature on Charlene left him dwarfed in silence and the consequence of that was that when he had to speak, he blurted it out with purpose, and then there were the genetics. I was not a big speaker, making big announcements, but Mum's DNA and the need to be confrontational ended up in my son's vocal chords when it mattered.

Then, of course, the moment that I had experienced with Lorraine would arrive with my own children. At some point the past would turn up, and growing up brought awareness and I was never without a photo of Lesley and nor was Mum, of course, so by the age of eight or nine, Chaz was asking questions and that really was the beginning and the oral history of our family started to be passed down. I know Charlene learned a lot from Mum and spent hours with her. Mum too, saw the same as I did. For Charlene, read Lesley.

Outside of our home, word got around about who we were and I couldn't know what Charlene was learning and which truths were mixed in with rumour, speculation and incomplete stories. We knew the facts within our walls, but there were still gaping holes in our knowledge – Smith's role and the undiscovered bodies being prime examples – but playgrounds can be nasty places and other kids of the same age get told only a fraction of the story. It was impossible to keep a lid on it.

I explained to my daughter what I wanted to, but I idolised her and wanted to protect her too – assuming I could find the words. One flick of Chaz's hair and it was Lesley standing before me. The resemblance was uncanny and for Mum, it marginally repaired her soul to see something close to what Lesley may have matured into.

Whether it is right or not, Charlene therefore largely self-educated herself about that day and its consequences. I told her what happened, but I rarely opened up to what I thought. I know it had a huge effect on them and whilst I was unable to really express myself to Charlene, Mum could. It is curious that it worked that way. We both saw Lesley in Charlene and I shut down for that reason, yet it seemed to set Mum free. I now realise too that every time I withdrew and gave very little detail, my own daughter probably had more questions for her Nana. Either way, it became the dominating theme of her upbringing, from the moment she was old enough to understand.

We lived with this tragedy always, and now the real psychological effects were clear, so for the chance for compensation to expire at three years and for people to still talk of closure they show no understanding of the stain and the scar that remain as the baton is passed from one generation to the next.

Then, as your own off-spring begin to understand the enormity of what has happened, despite being young still themselves, tragedy will strike again.

Chapter 19

Mum had spent much of the 1970s fighting. She took to radio phone-ins and TV shows whenever she could. It was both a coping mechanism and belief in the argument. By 1977 she was at loggerheads with Lord Longford. She had first encountered him in 1969, so soon after Lesley's murder. He had launched a campaign for Brady and Hindley's parole.

Not only had an inevitable death penalty been removed by the quirk of the calendar, but now life did not mean life at all. Within five years. That was their claim.

Mum had travelled to London to confront him, only to be palmed off with the invitation of a spot of lunch, while his secretary proceeded to tell her her how Myra Hindley was now a changed woman, a devout Christian and becoming an academic. Mum vowed to take him all the way. It felt a class battle – the haves against the have-nots. It seemed privilege against justice.

Eight years later a TV show called *Brass Tacks* aired from Manchester and the issue of parole had re-entered the public domain. A decade had passed since Hindley and Brady were sentenced. Mum agreed to appear – alongside a vice queen who had befriended Hindley in prison and Maureen Hindley. Longford was also on the panel.

My brother, Tommy, had escorted Mum to the show and, of course, there is the usual pre-show routine of green rooms and make-up, and one of the problems with a show like this is that you have to mix with the enemy. Longford approached Tommy, eerily addressing him with the same familiarity that Smith had confronted me with, outstretching his hand and greeting him on first name terms. Tommy blanked him and walked on by. Who, after all, would shake the hand of a man pitching the case for the freedom and re-assessment of Hindley's character?

Longford himself, as their mouthpiece, was a former cabinet minister, who fronted unpopular causes and spent huge amounts of time visiting many prisons – not just Hindley – and constantly arguing the case for reform. His default position seemed to be forgiveness, when surely you had to evaluate every single case on its merits and the individuals involved. You couldn't just call for blanket compassion, especially when it was only his word that Hindley was remorseful. Oh, and perhaps, the vice queen.

The Labour Prime Minister had described Longford as having the mental capacity of a twelve-year-old. He campaigned for pornography and to decriminalise homosexuality, only to later turn against the gay community.

His support for Hindley was largely mocked by the British press, who dubbed him 'Lord Wrongford'. It emerged that he had been in contact with her from her early days behind bars. He pitched her as merely an accomplice. Were they both crackers? Did Hindley see Longford coming and play him with this born-again religious card or was he using her for his own self-publicity? Or indeed, and likely, both.

The show began creepily with an appeal from inside Durham Prison, in which Hindley claimed it was unfair she had not been considered for parole and that she had done more than her time already for what she had been charged with, maintaining she was only in the room when Lesley was being tortured and was merely an accessory when Edward was being axed to death. She added that she could not show remorse for things she had not done. Astonishing words, really.

Outside of the 'panel' debate, the show invited callers. Hindley had always claimed that she was only still inside because of public opinion. Nothing wrong with that. Longford mocked some of the people who rung in and indeed hung up on them and these opinions included a nun who had visited Hindley inside and quashed the idea of the newly-reformed character that Longford was pitching. This was a woman of the church. Hindley was not. He also made short change of John Kilbride's father, who rang in to say that he would 'kill Myra Hindley if she ever gets out.'

The toll had exhausted the Kilbrides. Sheila and Patrick had divorced five years after their son was murdered. The fight was therefore both empowering and shattering.

Such was the hysteria around this show ten years on – and remember there was little media then (two main channels) and this case was still a one-off – that Maureen Smith's identity was protected on the night and she was whisked away under security straight after the show. I know Mum was gunning for her and by this point had no fear. A lot of time had passed since she had stood in Chester across from Brady and Hindley. Now, the cowardly mouthpiece and sister of the woman who took my sister was a few feet away in a TV studio. Mum was fearless.

I look back at the show with real affection. Mum told the watching audience that she too would kill Hindley if she were ever released. Both Mum and Pat Kilbride were putting down a marker. Why was this even being discussed? Within a decade we had gone from death penalty to parole for people like this? Those two parameters were vastly different, and ten years was not nearly enough to call forgiveness in such horrific cases.

The media is not for me and you can never measure how far you have come until time has passed, but I recall these years as Mum under medication and trauma, yet driven by justice and, when confronting it, she summoned strength from God only knows where. Even I, as her son, do not know where it came from. I had seen her slumped in a chair for six months without really going to bed, drugged up, but also waiting for Lesley to come home and here she was fighting it out on TV in an era when nobody was really all that media savvy, and frankly making fools out of these people.

After the show, Mum was rounded on by Janie Jones, the vice queen who had befriended Hindley in prison and still championed her cause, and Longford himself, who condemned Mum for not being able to forgive, implying that Christianity would reject her too if all she sought of Hindley was revenge.

It was extraordinary and if that is the definition of religion, then I am not sure I want a part of it.

With some lengthy absences, Mum was still at war with Longford in the 1980s. Even today, when you read it back, even if you have found God and forgiveness is your natural approach to life, can anyone really take a Lord seriously who appears on a TV debate with a vice queen and ten years on is calling for the release of Britain's most notorious female serial killer? If I said it was laughable, then that would be true, but it does not represent the exhaustion and the constant need to become that media-savvy person. Mum was learning fast to quash all the nonsense that emerges as the years pass and people forget a little, exaggerate a bit more and generally assume that the passing of time equals healing.

Our lives, therefore, were running in multiple identities. We would always be public even when the story had gone quiet. More often than not, it would be a media organisation who would find an angle to make events re-surface. The reality is that these were just moments. The struggle was real life and in 1979, we had to learn to cope once more.

Tommy and his first wife, Aileen, had come from hospital and were staying at ours after the birth of their son, Scott. At just five months old, they put him to bed one night and he never woke up again. We were now struck by the tragedy of cot death.

It wasn't even a case of 'just when you are getting back on your feet, disaster strikes' because some fourteen years after Lesley's abduction, it still felt like yesterday and when my brother discovered that little Scott had passed away in the night for no obvious reason, then it is impossible to proceed without that feeling that none of this is meant to be. We were a family cursed.

Scott was laid to rest next to Lesley.

And there was more to come.

Chapter 20

The consequence of that Boxing Day just never left us. The media's thirst for the story and the constant re-cycling of key dates and anniversaries meant that every year, even a decade or so on, you were still contacted for comment.

As time passed, that inevitably meant with death too. Those associated with the *Moors Murders* would in time pass away, completing the cycle, but re-opening the wounds. The first significant funeral came in 1980.

Mum received an anonymous call one night to say that Maureen Smith – Hindley's sister and wife of dodgy Dave Smith – had been admitted to hospital and had died of a brain tumour. Mum felt no compassion.

Whoever it was who chose to tip us off must have known what they were doing. I don't think they called because they felt we ought to know. I am sure it was the press goading for a response – to see if we would over-react, or give them a soundbite or turn up at Crumpsall Hospital.

There was one other significant detail. Myra Hindley had visited her under escort from prison, but had failed to arrive in time. This was actually a lot of information to take in in one go, but Mum was ecstatic that Hindley had not got there before she died and felt that was a justice that was deserved, given none of us had the chance to say goodbye to Lesley.

Even though Mum did not know who had called, she was extremely grateful for the knowledge, but it was the sign-off that left her troubled, but focussed.

'If they let her go to the hospital, they will let her go to the funeral,' the caller had said and then hung up.

It would have been quite intimidating, if it weren't helpful.

It was more than food for thought. It did not take long for Mum's temper to escalate. And these moments would come again for sure in the next few years. Mum was furious that rights were afforded to an individual who had deprived others of theirs – and those with a full life ahead of them like Lesley.

There was only one course of action. Mum would attend the funeral. Nor was she alone. John Kilbride's father had also received the same news and was not far behind. There had been no official confirmation that there *was* to be a service, but it became very obvious very quickly that this was happening, with police swarming around the crematorium, police dogs and CID on standby. It was a shocking waste of money and show of force – an over-reaction from the police. They were not there for Maureen Smith, whom hardly anyone remembered. They were there for Hindley, and their presence meant she was definitely coming.

And so it was. She stood there, flanked by burly guards, exiting a black limousine at haste, her blonde hair clearly identifiable. If anything, apart from the tip-off, the police presence was stupid because it drew attention that would not otherwise have been there.

Mum made her move towards Hindley, staring at her, then screaming in a rage, only to be restrained by an officer. Hindley eyeballed her back with the same icy stare she had displayed in court, making a mockery of everything Lord Longford had said about a changed woman who had found God. It was the same look, the same provocative hair and the same lack of remorse. Leopards didn't change their spots.

Mum had only the narrowest of opportunities to get to her and was aghast that the police were protecting Hindley. Why were they not helping *her*? And soon the moment had passed, with the doors of the crematorium closed and locked. Mum took this as a moment to break free from the police cordon and make her way to the side of the building, where she found the wreaths for collection after. One by one she went through them until she found what she was looking for – the card from Hindley to her sister. She set about destroying it, shredding every last leaf and petal.

Then, the police upped their game. Mum broke free with an aerosol spray in her hand trying to burn Hindley in the eyes, only to be manhandled once more, while yelling to be let free.

John Kilbride's father, Patrick, did manage to flee the officers and began rushing towards the cars, his eyes set on Hindley. He too was pinned to the ground, punched and kicked, as Hindley walked by ignoring him except for the fixed stare she now threw his way.

And then she was gone. The experience was satisfying, but frustrating too. Mum never thought she would get that close to her ever again, but having done so, felt the wheels of *in*justice that the protectors of the law defended someone who had broken it. You can understand of course that they had to do their job. This time there was no turning a blind eye as there had been when Alan and Mum went around to Smith's.

It set us all thinking of what the future might hold. If we had the information, these moments would surely come again.

But first, we nearly had to deal with another death in the family.

Chapter 21

Even at this point, fifteen years on, Mum was still heavily dependent on medication. It would stay with her until her dying day. Of course, much of what Mum had taken in over the years was intended to provide short-term solutions but became part of the norm, with inevitable side effects over the long term. A dependency had been created.

By 1981, I had split with Lorraine. We were too young and the spectre of the past just never went away. I was working nights as a casual worker and moved into a flat. I never thought I would ever be in this position. I behaved like I was single. Inside was a deep-seated feeling of self-loathing.

Charlene and Alan would come every other weekend and, whilst I missed both incredibly, it suited them. Invariably, I would end up taking them to my Mum's and, whilst Chaz hung on her every word for a while, consuming it all with Mum looking at her as though she was Lesley, my son Alan was quite disconnected, as if I had passed the gene on to him.

Mum was polarising though – she certainly didn't like my first wife Lorraine and it became very hard to have a relationship with her. I think it was territorial. Everyone except her Alan was regarded with suspicion – people were dangerous and she had spent all her of emotion over Lesley, so that meant expressions of love were in short supply, even if deep down she felt it. She was bitter but funny and I think the two went hand in hand. Sometimes when your emotions have been neutralised by such an awful experience, a dark wit emerges with a take on life that very few could share. That was Mum.

She never ever spoke of my Dad, except to say 'never marry a Catholic' and her relationship with Brett was strained at best. Being the youngest, I think he needed the most from her. He was born into this madness and inherited it young. *We* had some understanding of it from the moment it happened. We lived with the fallout.

I think he was always looking for guidance as he got older and it didn't really come as Mum was away with drugs, campaigning or just permanently emotionally exhausted. We had all known Mum before Lesley. Brett simply hadn't and Mum struggled with him. In fact she wasn't very nice to him and he spent a lot of time at mine. He was crying out for her love and it never came. Later when Brett was married and had five girls, she idolised them, but fell out with them too. Lesley's death cut through the generations. It cut way beyond those members of the family who lived it. Its knock-on effect would more than filter to the next generation and the one after that. Inability to love Brett properly and almost make him a scapegoat for being deprived of Lesley, meant that Mum tried harder with his kids and it came more naturally, but it also had the effect that once she got too close it would blow up in her face. A sniff of contentment would always be countered by the guilt that you would feel at pleasure. One person was not allowed to be there to experience joy – and that of course was Lesley.

I understand this because it was how I became. As much happiness as my children have brought me and I *have* been able to come out of my shell, it is the hardest thing to release yourself completely. You are constantly attending a party where the person whose party it is, hasn't turned up. It is very difficult to let yourself go unreservedly in those situations. And even though my own children have taken this on only anecdotally, it leaves a mental health scar throughout the DNA. Brett suffered more than most of us *in his head* too. The dislocation of time cost him dearly – being too young to understand at the time, but then being deprived of maternal love, took its toll and, like me going to sea, he had chosen flight, enrolling in the army for many years, probably to escape and definitely to experience a notion of family.

When he was away, he lost his eye. There are various stories as to what had happened according to who you talk to in the family. Some say that he had an accident whilst putting a light bulb in with the glass shattering in his face. Others say that he was in a fight and had been stabbed in the retina. The truth was that Brett had stabbed himself and had to wear a patch until a glass eye was fitted.

When he recovered and came home and married Marion, he withdrew even more. They were a very private family. He had fled because home never felt like that and when it was time to return, he became a recluse and you could never claim to know him. This is the knock-on effect of living without Lesley. Brett had so few memories of her, yet he picked up the pieces. Deprived of affection and attention, he had to forge his own identity whilst being permanently held back.

Mum was constantly on her guard, especially with the press. None of us were allowed to read a paper – that was where bad news and rumour lived. Yet, she knew how to play them and was so used to being in them that everyone stared at her when she went out. She became immune to the attention. I would regularly take the children to Rhyl in North Wales for holidays. One year, she invited the media and they were desperate for a picture of my children, so she authorised it as long as the headline read 'Protect These Children'. She had got wise to the power of print and she had learned how to meet them half way. For years, she was the subject of the glare of the lens, forever under the cosh, when less medicated and more understanding of the game, she became quite switched on and learnt how to trade, if you like.

That lack of emotion that she showed towards Brett did manifest itself positively into a no fear mentality. What, after all, did she have to lose? It meant selling your soul to the devil, in that if you asked the press for their help, then you waived all rights to privacy of course to give them the story. That meant that in the early 1980s, she contacted a reporter at *The People* to put her in touch with the medium, Doris Stokes.

This was desperation, but what was there to lose? I think, unless you are brought up with this kind of spirituality, most people only turn to such intermediaries when they are out of options and the fine line between common sense and fantasy has been crossed.

There *was* nothing to lose. So Mum and Alan took a train to London and met the journalist and made their way to Doris's house. They found a lady in her seventies who had been in this scenario many times before – as unique as our circumstances were, she recognised grief-stricken individuals hoping to cross over to the other side, without being able to make any guarantees herself.

Mum was transfixed, convinced that Lesley was talking to her directly through the words Doris was relaying. It is a very difficult one to call. Doris was a controversial figure, known in many parts of the world through TV shows, but associated with some grandiose claims that were often disputed – such as that she had helped the police solve murders. She was also hated by the church, who accused her of interfering with God's natural course and was outed for having plants in the audience of her shows. Some of it did look like a set-up. Mum was clearly an easy target, in that she was vulnerable, but also much of her story was in the public domain, so radiating an air of confidence about the facts was different – unlike Mum's previous experience directly after Lesley's disappearance, which turned out to resemble the truth, without any *known* evidence pointing in that direction at the time.

I am sceptical about what Mum relayed after. I am sure it sold a lot of newspapers. Lesley, via Stokes, was telling Mum she was fine and that Edward (Evans) wanted to say hello. To me, that is a red flag. If there is an afterlife, there are a hell of a lot of people in it and it does not necessarily follow that Lesley would even know the other victims. It is possible of course, but I think it is a very easy trick to pull. She didn't know Edward in 'real life' – dare I use the phrase.

Doris relayed that Lesley was spending her time amongst the babies and young children who had been taken too early and that she was upset about John, who had died in the routine operation. She had met a policeman who had worked on the case. She talked of Sunday School and family holidays. In fact she spoke exclusively of people who were known to the family. There were no wildcards, so to speak. The language relayed was what they call today a catch-up. But if it were real, you would think there would be new detail. Lesley would tell of experiences that we had no knowledge of. It was all a bit formulaic.

Mum said that there was some detail that she had to dig deep in her memory bank to authenticate but she left settled but unsure as to what to make of it. It gave her hope though that she would meet Lesley in Heaven. In time, Mum and her became friends and she took more and more heart from what Doris had said. The sealing moment came when Mum attended one of her shows without warning and Doris stopped, telling the audience that she was troubled by someone's presence in the venue only for her to then announce that this person was not there, but for Mum to raise her hand to confirm her presence. Doris welcomed her on stage with a bouquet from Lesley – none of which could realistically have been planned.

Who can ever know what to make of it? Some people have genuine skills and connections the rest of us cannot see or understand. Others like ourselves look to any form of comfort and spec of joy even when all hope has passed.

I think we were all living with this cloud of depression over us that would forever linger, so whilst I can take or leave the content, if the joy is a false dawn or one that will never see the light of day, then so be it. If our spirits are momentarily lifted then that, I think is fine. We have, of course, had a lifetime to mull it over.

Chapter 22

By 1982, I had met Linda. I don't know if I can honestly say that I was ready to settle down, but we are still together, have produced Terri in 1986 and Daniel in 1990 and I do know this: Second time around, I was going to have to think about how I would deal with all this now.

I had responsibilities in so many areas. I had to get off working nights for a start. Then we just had to find a way to manage with my older children living with their Mum, but descending into my new chaos.

But most importantly, I had to find a way this time. Whatever was going on in my head that I kept locked up there somehow had to get out. I don't know how I came across. I am not sure if those I knew just worked out when I was having a moment. People at work were aware, even though it had been many years. Colleagues just seemed to know. Apart from a few beers with the lads or football, I was never going to be the one to dominate a conversation. That just wasn't in my DNA. Lesley's death was in my early teens, so most people whom I came into contact with as an adult would only know me as just slightly withdrawn.

I understand this. I didn't ever really think about it then. You just live, don't you? You try to survive. Your mission is to silence those voices in your head that tell you every day about your role in all this – the brain obsessed with pressing eject on the movie that replays of the night I didn't go to the fair. Into the mix goes all the facts that I have absorbed third-hand from court – and much worse – the half-fact and rumour. All that speculation, tip-offs from journalists, notes through doors and the constant looks in the street were battling for airtime in my mind. Every single day.

It was always the same – the prominent themes never changed but when you see a Doris Stokes character on the news discussing this or other exchanges from beyond, you think of that element of the story. When you see Lord

Longford in a clip about something completely unrelated, you remember Mum's struggles. Horror movies you may have watched draw parallels. Maureen Smith's death makes you replay that 'doesn't he look like Lesley' moment over again and on it goes.

I had never really spoken about any of it, apart from to confirm that yes it was me and this was that family.

To that end, I owe Linda so much. We married two years after we met and I had to get it right. On so many levels. This kind of history of me was not something I wanted to be sharing onto a third marriage or more. I really had to put it out there and keep my counsel small.

Again, when do you introduce the narrative into your life? You know it is coming, she may be aware anyway, but you cannot just park it. Often there never seems to be a right time and then you just blurt it out. I think I waited a couple of months.

One day there was an item on the radio news about The Moors. This is the variable that I can never control. Somebody wants to talk about it when I am not ready. I am *never* ready but regularly, it becomes somebody's agenda and often through the years that was about Lord Longford's pushing his beliefs or Brady courting the media. That would so frequently be the angle. We had nothing new to offer. Lesley was still dead. We continued to grieve. The only developments could come from the perpretrators, fantasists, politicians or a random member of the public who suddenly believed they had fresh insight. There really was only one story that ever mattered until Brady and Hindley died – where the other bodies were and how many had there actually been?

I don't even recall what was being discussed that day. This often happened. Your subconscious hearing tunes, but then fades out too. You had been here too many times by the early 1980s.

But I took it as my moment to proceed through the traffic lights, and pull over. She hadn't known or realised, which I think gives you every indication that I had put a lock on it – wary of strangers, but also unable to communicate this massive demon in my head.

When I told Linda, the floor nearly swallowed her up. When you are in the first stages of courting and it is all glossy, new and lovely, you do not expect a bombshell like that. Nowadays, with so much more terrorism and awareness of it, we are less shocked and more exposed, so you can get into 'everybody knows somebody who knows somebody' territory. Not then. This was the crime of the century.

Once I started, I really couldn't stop – as though I would never let it out again in this detail. It was now or never. All or nothing. It was as though I had finally been given oxygen, and the breathlessness that anxiety can bring had temporarily passed. I felt exhausted by the time we got home. How can you even begin to do it all justice in a car journey? Then, of course, the conversation lingers a little over a few days and weeks. You remember a bit more, or feel capable of expressing a little deeper and that of course then provokes a whole new set of questions from Linda, some of which she probably still has not asked. To bring it all home a little more, Linda grew up in Gorton, not far from Pauline Reade's house.

If you love somebody, you have to share this stuff in your head. If you are loved back, it is unconditional to receive. You have a massive life decision to make as to whether you want be in the life and family where all this drama happens, but of course, if love prevails, there is no decision to be made. I never asked if it was too much for Linda, and she never said so.

We were who we were and nothing could change that. The rest lay ahead and so did building a future. Was I starting to find happiness? It was so hard to achieve. Things *were* on the up. I began to play football again on Sundays. Linda and I started to go to the Press club in Manchester, rolling in at 4 am or beyond. We were forever clubbing at *Madbreakers*!

I spent a lot of time with my cousin, Alan, and to find that genuine friendship in family helped immensely because we both understood and had it running through our veins, but

156

we just didn't have to talk about it in the opposite way to sometimes feeling that silent heavy awkward pressure that you do with people to whom you aren't as close to. It is odd how that works that those who don't know you so well feel the need to get it out the way and rarely succeed in doing so well.

In my cousin, I perhaps found some youth that I never had. Auntie Elsie and Uncle John's son and I lived every moment we could when were together, from football to drinking and clubbing. Sometimes we spilled over. I was a massive red and he worshipped City. Somehow our amazing friendship once ended up in a city centre brawl over a match and we were both whisked away by the police, bound for court. Dismissed by the judge, we just carried on messing about and, in Alan, I began to develop the happy-go-lucky chatty persona that I nearly had a chance to grow into so many years ago.

My relationship with my real Dad was improving too. He was now not far away, living just around the corner and was a real help decorating as we got to know each other a little more. We never spoke of Lesley and what happened and maybe I needed to with him more than anyone else. Perhaps he did too. Circumstance meant that he had been so detached physically from us and the events, but I am sure that being estranged made grieving worse. He was spared from press intrusion and the day to day battering, but he must have wanted answers first hand too. Lesley is his daughter. I could see the silent words in him that he too could see in me. We never really broke that down.

Did I know then that I had got lucky with Linda? Without a doubt, and I kept telling myself not to blow it.

That meant too that I still had a lot of it locked inside my head but, for the first time, I was able to speak openly, but in a limited way and begin to make some sort of therapeutic sense.

One thing that is clear in my mind is that if I had not found Linda, I may never have found myself.

Chapter 23

By 1985, Brady was conversing with almost anyone who would listen. If you would give him an audience, then he would use you to attempt to influence the narrative.

He reportedly confessed to the *Sunday Times* that he had also been responsible for the murders of Pauline Reade and Keith Bennett. The police had long since believed this – their disappearances bore all the hallmarks of a Brady swoop – their locality and timing so close to the others.

Who can possibly know what Brady wanted to achieve by choosing this moment two decades on? Was it borne out of boredom, glory-hunting, self-image ...who can know? Every time something like this happened, it just started it all again. Greater Manchester Police re-opened the case. The media re-ignited their interest.

Already by the middle of the 80s, we were in a much different Britain – a country whose issues now included mass unemployment, the closure of the pits, a recent war in the Falklands, AIDS, football violence, including bans and deaths at home and in Europe. A whole new generation were now learning of what happened on The Moors before they were born and this was the Britain they were born into, where grim was a lot more commonplace.

Whilst we of course wanted the best outcomes for all the families this buzz of activity was stifling. It was too much for my own Dad, who had had enough of its constant presence and had moved to North London to escape it all – and he was rarely under media scrutiny, but still haunted by being in its slipstream.

I went quiet again. You didn't really believe there could be new intelligence about Lesley, but by now we knew well many of the other relatives and every fresh detail we shared and lived through, as though we were getting the call back then twenty years previously. For the Reade and Bennett family, I don't know what fresh set of emotions this brought.

Their children still hadn't come home. They suspected this was at the hands of Brady. There remained no location of a body. You may think again that this gives some sort of closure and cries of 'finally', but I can tell you that waiting two decades to hear what could have been said back in court at Chester only makes your blood boil more and when you think you have learned to deal with it over, the process re-sets itself. I can assure you that there is no 'ah well, at least we know for definite now' about this.

It looks as though Brady wanted his moment. When the police went to visit him in July 1985, he mocked suggestions that he had confessed. The police really had nowhere to go – except back to Saddleworth, using Hindley's photography to cast fresh eyes on the scene.

It was not quite open season on Brady, but he was certainly willing to engage. It is well documented that Winnie Johnson's repeated wish was *just* to know where her son was buried. Both she and Mum re-joined the circus. Both considered writing to the killers.

By now, Hindley was being held in Kent and Brady was in Leicestershire, but about to be moved to Ashworth High Security Hospital on Merseyside after being diagnosed as a psychopath. It took this long to come to that conclusion. Hindley did at least agree to study the photos and topography of the land in a bid to help them identify the likely terrain.

It is difficult to say if, free from Brady, she had changed and repented. She did still maintain her innocence regarding Pauline and Keith. But she had been banging the changed woman drum – or getting others to do it for her – almost since she was first imprisoned.

Mum's lifelong mission since the sentencing of Brady and Hindley was simple. She wanted to help every other mother out there and she would fight to the death to ensure that they both stayed inside. Perhaps this was behind Hindley's willingness to appear repentant and assist, whereas Brady was more intent on toying. It looked like there might be dialogue with Hindley and that could cast her in a more favourable light

159

especially to a new 'audience' of a different generation and an ever-changing set of politicians. For Brady, the game from the tormenting controlling mind of the psychopath was very much still on and the article, despite his subsequent denials, seemed to have woken the sleeping monster.

Mum was desperate to know one other thing. Even though it had been two decades and she had heard the recording of Lesley being tortured, she still wanted to know if Lesley had suffered. It seems obvious that she did. I don't know really why this was so important. Obviously, we know the end, so it seems definite but she held this tender craving, out of maternal instinct, that her last moments were without pain – clutching perhaps to a straw similar to those offered by Doris Stokes.

So, in March 1986, she took the plunge. She wrote to Brady, with the help of the BBC, who were keen to participate, in the hope of making a TV show.

She asked him straight. Would the two of them meet?

To my astonishment – at both Mum and Brady – he replied that he would, upon certain conditions. Mum duly accepted, but then had to wait an eternity for a further reply. I don't know if the letter was intercepted or if the idea was a non-starter, or if him killing time was also part of the plan. Brady had all the time in the world.

Mum only wrote to Hindley once. Hindley wanted to be seen to co-operate and did not seem to be playing the same games as Brady. There must have been something going on behind the scenes – some sort of rumblings across the media, the politicians and parole system. The BBC approached Mum, after all. The suggestion that Mum and Brady would meet seemed crazy.

By December 1986, Hindley did return to the Moors, flown in by police helicopter – the sort of arrival in that location that would certainly indicate an official search and, for many, that only meant one thing. The police ensured a media blackout at the time, though it was subsequently reported. If it had been common knowledge, it would not have been possible. To our generation, a chill still ran down your neck at the mention of their names and there would have been a queue a fair way behind Mum and Alan waiting to greet her. Some 135 officers, including a decoy party, were both protecting Hindley and leading the search.

They found nothing.

By 10 February 1987, Hindley had confessed to all five murders and also exonerated her brother-in-law, David Smith. Brady and her were now poles apart in their agendas – perhaps some explanation for the delay in replying to Mum.

The confession lasted seventeen hours, running to 700 pages and is held in the National Archives, but cannot be accessed until 2072, which serves no real purpose to anybody. But her words fell short. She still maintained that at every killing, she was in the car, over the brow of the hill or in the bathroom or kitchen. Even these scarce details were kept from the public for a month. This is either an unlikely truth or Hindley's game was very different – full steam ahead for parole. The posturing had begun.

By April, Lord Longford was pleading her case, writing that 'mob emotion' only was being satisfied in detaining her. Wow, what a statement.

Were five the final total of bodies? Was it the total number of attempted abductions? Were there others who didn't want the spotlight, who simply had not come forward at the time? She did not confess to more at the time.

The police were now back on the Moors in earnest, re-combing as much as was humanly possible so long after. At huge cost and a drain on resources, the possibility of a wild goose chase was high – not because Hindley was bluffing, but because of the landscape.

Eventually, after three months, on 1 July 1987, the body of Pauline Reade was found. She lay just around 100 metres from Lesley.

As I write those words, I shudder. For Lesley, for Pauline, for not finding her all those years ago and for all the lies since. I think it follows that unless a body has been displaced by weather or animals, then you would have a pretty good idea if you had 'buried' two so close to each other. You didn't really need a map. All Hindley had to do was to say that Pauline was near Lesley and you would hope that the rest would fall into place, so while it *appears* that Hindley had changed and wanted to show some remorse by the mid 80s, those claims and those made by Lord Longford so soon after sentencing are clearly ridiculous.

Two days later, the police took Ian Brady to Saddleworth. He had been toying with Detective Topping for some time, but made a formal confession after the discovery of Pauline Reade's body *and* a statement to the press saying that he would assist the search. Serial killers are fond of their trophies when they are on the run. When they are caught, they often crave full acknowledgement. It seems that 'the new' Hindley may have been one step ahead of Brady and he was forced to play catch up. Hindley and Brady had long since split ranks.

The time between Pauline's body being found and Brady's statement is miniscule. The visit to the Moors on 3 July seems sensationally quick on that basis. This time, the press, unsurprisingly *were* there. By three in the afternoon, they had found nothing and abandoned the search, denying Brady further visits. He had his only chance. Now, finally Brady did pick up the pen and write, but it wasn't immediately to Mum. He sent a letter to Peter Gould at the BBC, the producer who was trying to initiate their meeting in the first place. He stated that there were five additional victims, but gave no other information. Hindley played dumb. The Director of Public Prosecutions also decided that there was nothing to be gained in a trial to account for Pauline and Keith. Increased airtime for either party could also help their cause, especially for Hindley seeking parole.

Brady did return to the moor that December, but could not locate the graves. By August 1987 the police had abandoned the search officially. Still there was no Keith, nor would there ever likely be now without a chance intervention.

Chapter 24

All this proves that over twenty years on, there is still no escape. In time, I could draw comparisons with the victims of Hillsborough. So much time would pass in life before they had any sense of justice, hoodwinked by the system, corrupt officers and a press willing to write their own lies, regardless of the grief that it piled upon the original trauma.

And 1987 – two years before that tragic Saturday afternoon in Sheffield – seemed to be the year when everything started to gather momentum again. There is no doubt that Hindley's confession triggered everything, but equally there were a group of individuals who still found political capital in what happened. Also, we were a further generation down the line and sometimes that could suggest compassion and forgiveness, with no context to the brutality and rarity of what Brady and Hindley did. In short, if you fell for the new-born Hindley, you might well think she should be released.

But this is why people like Mum get dubbed lifelong campaigners, because for every moment that Hindley remained alive, there was a chance of release and that kept Mum on guard, on a nervous edge no less, waking up every day thinking about it. You do not choose to be a lifelong campaigner. One day simply follows another and before you know, it is *lifelong.* Once you start the process, as Hillsborough shows, you are in it forever. Nor do you have a choice.

In terms of her parole, I don't really know if the decision-makers of the day were tuned in to the thoughts of the families. I do hope that they didn't think it was all forgotten, because I can assure you that – as Maureen Smith's funeral confirmed – the moment Mum could get to Hindley, then she would. Nor was she alone. I know that I can count several other victims' relatives on that list. You could never rule out a crazed member of the public either, who might make their own justice or spot her in the street, report it to the press with unknown consequences – not that I am trying to protect Hindley.

What I do know is that maternal love for her own children was actually something Mum was not really capable of because of these two. She showed her love, but it was to other mothers. Fighting to keep Hindley inside and playing games with Brady was a love without affection, but a commitment of passion to Lesley and every mum on the planet.

Whilst it is fair to say that I missed out, even though Mum knew that I was torn to pieces by not going to the fair, I have to accept that. When I look back, I saw a dutiful, determined woman who would not let up and, despite what the medication had done to her, somehow there was a space in her brain that the pills and tablets had freed up and energised, leaving her to fight on and often against her old enemy, Lord Longford.

It wasn't just his re-emergence and Hindley's confession that made this year pivotal. Pauline's mother, Joan Reade was admitted to Springfield Mental Hospital in Manchester. She, like Mum, had to be heavily sedated and was just about able to attend Pauline's funeral that year. We all had experienced that wait for official news. Coping strategies were all we had and they were no more than that. To have this thrown back at you as Hindley decides to confess over two decades later for her own gain, probably means that the 20 plus you learned to cope, go straight out of the window. It can't be a co-incidence that, in the year Pauline was discovered, her Mum breaks down and to that level.

It was also in 1987 that Manchester City Council decided to demolish the house on Wardle Avenue where Brady and Hindley had lived. In effect, this was the last place Edward Evans and Lesley were alive. How do you evaluate something like that? There is no place for that building in society. Who would ever want to live there? But, it remains the last place that my little sister saw. The council blamed 'excessive media

164

interest' that created unpleasantness for the residents. Or perhaps, they found a bit of class and taste? The problem is that once a property like that survives a couple of generations, then it becomes a tourist trap – unbelievable, I know, that murder and death attracts the dark in individuals, but it does. One of the most visited places today is the 9/11 Memorial in New York.

Mum wrote to Hindley in that August. She had read that she wanted to broadcast an apology on the radio to the parents of the victims but it had been vetoed. Hindley replied and I can remember Mum turning into a rage when she opened the letter. Once again, it was all about self-preservation and denial and image-building with Hindley stating that 'your child was not physically tortured'. This clearly was nonsense. Mum had heard the tape once and that was more than enough.

I don't know if Hindley wrote that suspecting it might reach a wider audience, as in the press, or if she thinks Mum was stupid. Or, if her mind had gone walkabout and she no longer could remember the brutal facts. Mum shook of course as she read her words – as she did with Brady. To know that she was holding prison paper that had their DNA all over it was harrowing enough before you digested their content. I have those letters now. I touch them rarely. It is still an uncomfortable moment.

Brady had at least entered into discussion with Mum – principally about parole, which was not his, but Hindley's motivation. He, playing the controlling intellectual, was willing to meet, but without cameras, in total privacy and away from doctors and guards. He never mentioned parole for himself. Hindley had been told that she would spend 25 years behind bars before being eligible. In 1985, the Home Secretary, Leon Brittan, increased it to 30 years. You can see therefore why the issue was bubbling in the late 80s. The Prime Minister, Margaret Thatcher, believed these sentences were too short and that neither should ever be released. At least, politicians were staying the course.

Mum also received letters and flowers from the Kray Twins, which was just totally bizarre. They were also inside. None of us could get our heads around this criminal fraternity that wanted to befriend victims. A sick game and part of the control, or genuine repentance? We were always likely to conclude the former. Jimmy Saville had also visited Brady. However big your ego and fame was, before his own scandal, why would you even do that?

Brady wrote several times to Mum. He knew he had an audience. He was probably smart enough to know that if he gave Mum a bit, it might have legs and, as I sit here now, touching the same manky prison papers, just for the sake of this chapter, with equal vile in my stomach, I see he was adamant that Dave Smith – the man who remarked how like Lesley I was – had been the major beneficiary of a cover-up. We had all suspected this, of course and Brady may well have been aware that Hindley had exonerated him in his confession.

It was almost impossible to know what to believe. Hindley and Brady's relations were soured from as far back as 1972 when amazingly she had written to him to say it was all over – as if there were any chance of getting back together. Characters like Lord Longford were muddying the waters.

Mum had called Longford, amidst all this furore about parole and Hindley's confession. This took some balls – on an earlier TV show, she had already called Hindley 'the devil's daughter' and Lord Longford 'the devil's disciple'. Mum had been storing stuff up and had parked him in her mind, but the anger over the revelations of two further bodies had prompted the call. Longford replied that Mum was eaten away with hate, insisting still that 'Myra was a good catholic girl'. Then he backtracked, inviting Mum for drinks.

Muppets like him really did not help and the class divide, which in his make-believe world of fantasy power, where a few pulled strings could do the trick, was as sickening as the acts themselves that he was defending. To fall foul of evil controlling serial killers was the worst nightmare. Justice had been served on those two. To run into people championing

166

their cause was vomit-inducing. This was just another phone call in his pompous Westminster world. To us, it meant you could never go forward. You were always fighting something and then you are left fighting yourself with depression and anxiety, which just never go away.

One other thing bugged Mum. There was often a lot of media about luxury conditions at maximum-security prisons. This irritates normal people, not just the victims, whose perpetrators are inside. But this had been rumbling with Mum since 1972 when it emerged that Hindley was a Category B prisoner and was able to go for walks in the parks. It had only been a few years and she was being given this much freedom, already prompting Mum to write a three page letter and forcing a debate in parliament. It must have had some effect on Hindley, because the following year she tried to escape from Holloway, having hatched a plan with her new lesbian inmate lover, Patrician Cairns, to flee to Brazil to become a missionary. So, Longford was right! She had found God, but only because he had the airline tickets.

Despite being quite far down the line, to the extent that a forged driving license in the name of Myra Spencer had been found at the lover's flat, the plot was foiled and Cairns was jailed for five years.

Now years later, Mum and Alan decided to head to Cookham Prison down south. This was where Hindley was being held at the time. They would see for themselves.

You have to admire Mum's acquired media know-how. This was not part of her. She learned as she went. So, with her was a photographer from the press and that tells you that she wasn't doing this on impulse. She was planning with strategy.

They entered the grounds of the jail and refused to move, despite being confronted. Word would certainly reach Hindley that Mum was there. That was entirely her intention with the snapper in tow. Wardens tried to move Mum on, knowing full well who she was, but also gave her the nod to say that Hindley knew they were there. How this had got round the prison so quickly is beyond me. Perhaps the officer's language was protocol – standard to anyone trying to infiltrate.

These acts may seem reckless. Who really thinks they can penetrate a prison wall?! Just my Mum. That wasn't the purpose. Mum wanted Hindley to know that, for her, all noise and posture, she would be stalked until the day she died. Job done.

You would think that after 20 plus years, you could become immune or just walk away from it, but our lives were split into a new DNA that was already rubbing off on our children. For Mum, the effects were obvious. A life of stress, pills and fight were killing her. For me, I was lost inside my mind and Lesley's death in something I just didn't understand at the time. For our children, the story came round full circle.

In simple terms, once you deal with her disappearance you manage her loss. Then you have the body, the trial and the realisation that you are in a family of other families that nobody wanted to be cast in. Grief plateaus, but still sits on your shoulder. Then, other people stick their nose in – from conspiracy theorists to documentary makers, politicians to mediums. When they have had their say, other people respond and finally you get Brady weighing in to make sure the truth is perfect for his own legacy, but countered by Hindley distorting all opinion, emotion and fact in her bid for parole.

So, when people say after 20-plus years, did you not start (surely?) by then to deal with it, the answer remains no. As much as Linda became the only rock I ever had and the unique opportunity to express myself in the absence of counselling, you have to understand that it is everyone else who label it as '20 years plus' (at that point). For me, and for the family, yesterday was always Boxing Day and tomorrow never came. We lived life on a daily basis, coping and fighting and dealing with it. To us, there was no concept of two decades or so passing.

It was always yesterday.

Chapter 25

After years of nothingness, with very little happening in the 1970s, Mum was consumed by dialogue. That Brady had responded to her gave her hope. I am not sure what that hope was. Perhaps, it is as simple as thinking you would get the last word and that the final page of the history books would depict events as you saw them and not as a controlling psychopath tried to dictate them.

Once Brady began communicating, it opened all sorts of possibilities. None of us had been ready for that visit from Smith at our house and they had addressed that by beating him at his flat and I know Mum and Alan were quite capable of tracking him down again. To them, he was pathetic compared to Brady.

Instead, they focussed on an unusual target. Brady's Mum.

Alan and Mum made their way round to see her in Chorlton-on-Medlock, with no ounce of aggression or pre-determined hostility that they bore when they visited Smith. I suppose Brady's Mum had suffered too, but when they arrived they were anticipating a half-blind frail old lady who had rarely been seen in public. All that most people knew of her was from a minimal media-based description. Instead they found a firm, confident woman who seemed in good health.

It gave Mum focus to engage with these people – a wrestling back of control, where any victories were hollow ones. I suppose it also took courage to confront, but Mum had become fearless when it came to Lesley. Whilst I fought with it all my life in my head, she felt that dialogue was the best way forward, however surreal the circumstances.

Having tea with Mrs Brady was not for me. I would just check in a week later and pick up the pieces of the conversation. In a way, Mum's relentless pursuit of those responsible and those championing the causes made me more withdrawn. I couldn't really talk about any of it, apart from a little to Linda and to confirm small bits to the kids as they got older, but Mum could express herself better and it was less locked in her mind than myself because confrontation was more in her genes.

I can not imagine having tea with any Brady, regardless of whether or not they were involved. For me, if that was your son then you were involved. Mrs Brady too – it seems – had not bit into the media circus, claiming to have never read any of the papers and not be aware of any of the detail Mum and Alan told her that day. She was exchanging letters with her son and presumably had been to see him, but what their level of detachment against engagement was like, nobody could really know. You are never prepared for your own child going to prison and in these circumstances.

Nor can I imagine what it must be like to have chosen to have blocked out all the coverage for over two decades, only to be then told the truth. If indeed that was true. Today, I am sure that you would be straight on the internet, rewinding the clock and googling the night away. Back then it was different, but her media blackout surely must leave you wondering what everyone has been saying all these years. Twenty years is a long time to bury your head in the sand.

As Mum and Alan left, agreeing in principle to meet a second time for tea, photographers were at the door. Word had spread that Mrs Brady had visitors, but I think it shows that Alan and Mum bore no animosity to her, because their instinct was to protect *her* from the snappers, ushering her back inside, whereas they had been used to it for years.

If control was king for the psychopath, Mum had taken it back slightly from Brady. The visit to his mother meant that he now began replying to Mum's letters more readily, teasing Mum that she would be soon reading about new developments – a cruel thing to say, but one which reclaimed power and inflicted more pain on a nervous system shot to pieces.

Remember – he is writing his letters as the police are searching The Moors for the first time in years. He knows what is in his head and probably where bodies are, but he can't legislate for the outcome of the searches, especially if Hindley has been helping. Mum could read between the lines and strongly believed that the publicity Hindley was getting had severely wound up Brady. Also, talking to his mother was an angle nobody had previously considered. Amidst all the noise and bravado, the little child inside the killer perhaps still craved some maternal approval from the rubble of his own messed-up childhood.

At times the correspondence would play games, at others it would bemoan at his fatigue at the searching of the moors. Sometimes too, he seemed to open up to Mum – or was he just trying to get a message through? He definitely wanted to take Smith down with him, but he also confessed to four further murders, including two in Scotland. The police did nothing about this, insisting that it was part of Brady's game. It is so difficult to know which truth is the real one – was he using Mum for his own legacy or to get at Hindley or can a mentally ill man actually feel that the mother of one of his victims is now his confidante, based on a cup of tea with his own Mum? Were these signs that he was mentally ill – or that he was more than all there?

I shake my head and shudder. It is too much to think about, and again this is the knock on effect that when you start to engage and then get into the head of the serial killer then your own becomes battered as a pattern starts of second-guessing, over analysing, which in turn furthers your anxiety, compulsive disorder and depression.

The talk of bodies in Scotland made some sense – he was born there. Equally, Brady would be happy to throw the police a wild goose chase and hang Hindley out to dry.

None of us ever heard any more about Scotland, until an article in 2011. It is always going to be a question asked of serial killers – how many were there? But it seems that Brady confessed to another inmate, who was about to be released and head off north of the border, bragging that a month prior to The Moors Murders, he had carried out a contract job at Loch Lomond for the underworld of Glasgow, before visiting the sights. He had also several armed robberies planned. If true, it portrays him in a slightly different light – one is a gangster who will kill anybody off if the job is right; the other is the meticulously planning child killer, whose methods include slow torture and sexual gratification. But they were, of course, members of that gun club and Brady also went on to say that if he had known they were going to be captured then he would have got his guns out for a fire fight with the police until the last man was standing.

In 1988, Brady was at his most prolific in writing to Mum, triggered by the discovery of Pauline Reade's body, but obsessing about the detail and the accuracy of the reporting. He *was* using Mum because Hindley was coming across as helpful with her reported to be having hypnosis in prison to help identify Keith's grave, whereas he seemed obstructive and his adamant stance that he had killed in Scotland was still receiving short change from the police. He seemed intent on getting Mum to put it out there so that he could take the credit for those and additional murders in the Manchester area, which he had begun to attach himself to when Scotland fell on death ears.

It is almost like a scene from a movie that Mum was getting all this information – whether true or not. It did not add to her grief. She was already beyond numb, but what did rile her was when Brady attempted to exchange polite pleasantries, as if the volume of correspondence and her contact with his own Mum had given him carte blanche to do so. Mum did not want letters asking how she was etc. She just wanted facts and a meeting.

Brady lent on her, bemoaning how his medication had dropped and citing police cover-ups and PR gimmicks. I hold the letters now as I write this and I see shaky graphology, obsessive stream of consciousness and aggressive underlining of key points that he wants to make. There is not an ounce of remorse. He had resorted to calling his ex-partner simply M.H. Mum would simply reply by sending newspaper cuttings back to him. She had more than learnt to play the game.

172

But perhaps Hindley was playing it best of all – much of Brady's issues following the discovery of Pauline's body was that Hindley's technique was to help the police to get to the vicinity of the graves, but then feign ignorance when (as Brady claims) she knew exactly where the bodies were buried. It was a front to appease the Parole Board. It is much easier to see the game from here in 2018, as I write, rather than as it unfolds in real time, but Brady's and Hindley's sour love had become a power struggle and we were all in it. The more she got publicity, the more he would write to Mum.

As you can expect the reading of these letters today is distressing. I see Mum's fight and determination that I had become a little detached from, in that I was only really at hers with my kids at the weekend – plus I had to try to make something of life and the children were my priority. At the time, Mum didn't have long left to live and maybe knew so.

This therefore became her dying wish. But just holding these letters today in 2018 still puts you on a one to one with their writer. I hold paper touched by the man who murdered my sister. I read a little and stare into space. I see Brady and he therefore gets into my head. I have no words again. They are pounding the inside of my skull. I shake my head and my body shakes too. I don't know if I am angered at the arrogance of him communicating at all or exhilarated for Mum that she could have dialogue and seemed to be 'winning'.

And this now after all this time. I have been up to the loft for them rarely – perhaps stared at them a handful of times. Compare that to the moment they arrived through the letterbox and the adrenaline rush of fear and excitement that would have filled Mum, followed by us standing around reading her facial expressions and waiting to hear what he had written, before going back over it again to make sure. That trepidation at opening the envelope causes shaking. You never quite take in the words the first time you read the letter, so you try a second time and then ask someone else to read it. Then you analyse it in your head and out loud, taking a few other opinions and you pace the room like you did the night Lesley did not come

173

home. You sob, you bang fists, you feel anger and disgust, but then you find some positive, in that there does seem to be a willingness to engage and if the volume and tone of correspondence had been borne out of Hindley's assistance in finding Pauline's body, then you have to keep banging that drum to work Brady for the sake of Keith.

Everybody had their own agenda. Mum didn't know which bits were true and which weren't, but one particular aspect of the correspondence stayed with her – there was collusion between the press and the police and the concept of cover-ups for the latter never left her.

Chapter 26

I have come to realise that whilst there is a constant drip-feed and renewed curiosity about The Moors Murders, years like 1987 and 1988 were peaks – simply because of Hindley's confession and the subsequent search of The Moors.

The reality is that these moments were for other people – the villains, the press, the police, the politicians and the public – all of whom, without exception were having their fifteen minutes of fame. Many of these people were kind and did a good job. A small percentage did revel in it. Little did we know that in the 1990s a young woman called Caron Foley or Caz Telfer was absorbing all of this. She became a by-product of that gory glory that some voyeurs found in this tragic story.

For the families, there was perhaps comfort and certainly distress at Pauline's body being found but Keith's not. For us, our stop start life had to go on. Linda and I had to concentrate on our relatively new additions in Terri and Daniel, plus of course Paul from Linda's previous marriage. We always struggled financially and the house was constantly full, but the noise was a welcome antidote to the heavy atmosphere I had grown up with and now I had my own I needed to try to build some sort of happy home. I knew this was my only chance at it and, even though I was still very reserved but with a good sense of humour, I had to set an example in my family where often I had little history of the same to take my lead from.

With Linda by my side, I found strength to be happy – and as awkward as that sounds, it was always a building bricks process…bit by bit, day by day until the next thing would set you back a little.

In late August 1990, there was that familiar knock at the door.

'Terry Downey?' they asked, knowing.

It was the police.

They had come to tell me that my father had passed away. We were both Terry Downey, even though I had taken the name West many years before. For once, this was a visit from officers that bore bad news that was almost acceptable in that it hadn't come in tragic circumstances. But, of course, we were all devastated and made for North London as soon as we could, with my Uncle Jimmy and Auntie Pat. Linda had to remain at home – what a time to be 39 weeks pregnant.

At some point, most people have to make those car journeys similar to this. There were long periods of silence and disbelief and some of smiling and laughing at happy memories. It hit me when we pulled up and Uncle Jimmy asked me to carry the flowers to the house. It really hit me – because I didn't know Dad was ill.

And now, I am holding a huge cross that will lay on the top of his coffin.

Then as we bury him, I have so many thoughts. So many times I have said goodbye to loved ones in appalling circumstances. Now, I reflected on those losses again and my Dad's relationship with those people – Lesley, of course – and how difficult being estranged must have been too.

Then, obviously, I realised that he was gone and knew that our own relationship was one that we never really had. I am not the first to be in the position and wonder why we hadn't bridged the gap more, whilst understanding that now it was too late.

And it wasn't just me – Charlene was the eldest grandchild, but had refused to go in the funeral car, then wouldn't get out of any vehicle when we arrived. We have discussed it since. The explanation is obvious. Not only was she distraught at the loss of her Granddad, but she too was upset for the man she hardly knew.

These were feelings in my daughter that hadn't just swelled at our loss. I hadn't really considered them until this point. It was a clear marker as to some issues that lay ahead – proof once more that events of 1964 cut through at least the next two generations.

That aside, the early 90s were probably the quietest time since 1965. Campaigners and aggravators like Lord Longford no longer had a voice. There were unlikely to be any more searches of The Moors, so that oxygen of publicity was extinguished, and Mum really was starting to fade.

The crushing blow for Myra Hindley came in 1990 when the Home Secretary confirmed that life meant life – even though we had already heard this several times, which meant that even this could be a meaningless statement that a subsequent government might overturn. We read it as 'life means life – for now'. Interestingly, and I do not know the reasons, but I learned that Hindley was not told of this decision until four years later. In a way that feels like a justice that she must have been hanging on hoping for parole after the searches in 1987 and 1988. Hindsight lets you understand now that even though we didn't see it at the time, there must have been a groundswell for it to have even been put before the Home Secretary and her attempts to force a ruling seem to have been successful *and* as a direct result of her confession and own publicity campaign – if I can call it that. Sickening, really.

Every time Mum had this news confirmed, it meant that she could back off the fight a little. Job done for now. Lesley's memory was preserved. Imagine though that as the years go by and Mum fights several times to keep Hindley behind bars, if as Mum neared the end of her best years, a Home Secretary had reversed that situation. Years of campaigning and then when you think you can go to your own grave yet *she* might walk freely, that was what kept Mum on edge and on her guard every single day.

It is extraordinary to think that by the mid 90 s a day that always just still felt like yesterday was now actually 30 years previous. Let's talk about that closure thing again. No – it is never going to happen. The Moors stay with you forever in so many ways, from the stance that administrators take towards to you, to the grief that is embedded in your entire family, including the next generations.

177

In terms of that officialdom, Mum and Alan had wanted to adopt and having got so far down the lengthy process were knocked back because of Lesley. They were criticised for not mentioning it in the process and for it being the reason their home might not be a stable environment. What on earth are you supposed to do about that? Mum did desperately want a little girl – not to replace Lesley, of course – but I think to help her feel maternal and feminine.

All of her kids – myself especially – became over protective about our own playing out and setting home times. Chaz often didn't get the answers from me she needed about the past, so forged a close relationship with Mum, but at times I could see that was fraught with tension. Is this what the adoption services were alluding to? That the closeness of love that Mum and my daughter could have because of the void of Lesley also meant that nobody could fill it. You could get close – very close – but you would never be Lesley, so emotions could be full on and natural, but then take a step back because you can't share that mental load.

Nothing exemplifies this more than what happened on three separate occasions from 1994 onwards – annually to the day, and that day was Lesley's birthday. Lesley's grave was desecrated. She lay two rows in front of Edward Evans, as chance would have it. The plot had remained intact and respected for three decades. Now, in what did not look like a coincidence, it was vandalised three years running.

Crazy members of the public can do this – but could a family member? Sometimes tensions ran so high that nobody knew what to believe and in the end Mum decided that it was Charlene who had done this.

Why would she? Sometimes you lash out and a lifetime of second-guessing means that you no longer know your own mind and take it out on those whom you love. Lesley's death affected us all, even the next generation, but we were all united in our love for her. She was too young, innocent and pure to think anything bad of her. All of our memories were sweet and joyous. Nobody in the family felt the need to crave that much attention that they would attack her grave, not once, but three times, and on what would have been Lesley's birthday.

It showed that Mum's brain was split between the shrewd and the broken. The willpower to fight councils over housing, Hindley over parole and Longford over his dated pomposity was where her brain focussed, but there wasn't much left for the day to day. Charlene did not desecrate that grave. Even discussing it was a bad idea because it simply meant that whilst you were accusing, somebody else was getting away with it.

Charlene *had* been to the grave on the morning of Lesley's birthday to leave flowers, as she always did. She was followed a couple of hours later by Elaine, the daughter of John and Elsie who discovered its sorry state. Chaz was, of course, devastated. Mum wanted someone to blame. I think it is hard to understand perhaps there is no escaping that Lesley dominated our lives and that is both in grief and a restriction in emotional expression, but also in the responsibility that we all shared as a family, whether you were born after her death or not.

Way before Charlene was an adult, Lesley's death resonated with her. It didn't matter that she wasn't alive at the time. It was part of the family story – glue that just about held us together, whilst tearing us apart. Even if you were born into it, the sentiments transferred so Charlene, therefore, was as proud as anyone to lay flowers at her place of rest.

Mum couldn't prove that Charlene hadn't done it and Charlene couldn't convince her otherwise and even though it was quite ridiculous to suggest so, I think you can sense that when Mum got an idea in her head, stubbornness prevailed and it was hard to remove it. You would get the corner of the eye look where nothing was being said, but her pupils were radiating suspicion, as if the unspoken words were 'how can I be sure you are telling the truth'?

The reality is that Lesley's grave now bore the words 'Myra is living' and 'Free Myra Hindley. Your daughter's bones are going to be dug up and put back on The Moors

179

where they belong, unless you keep your mouth shut about Hindley'.

What on earth are we supposed to think? Firstly, and obviously, if Chaz craved some sort of attention, which she didn't, then her language would not be about keeping quiet on Hindley, nor would she be so coarse and aggressive about Lesley's remains. Most importantly though, this just underlines our belief that, whilst most people are kind-hearted, a few are attracted to the drama. And for every Brady out there, who knows how many wannabes fed off his story?

The world has had and still has enough serial killers and copycat killers for me to know this opinion is true. What worries me is that I do not believe that whoever wrote this rubbish and dismantled all the flowers actually had anything to do with Hindley's freedom. It wasn't Lord Longford's cronies, for Heaven's Sake.

I am sure it was just a gang of youths being idiots – and to a new generation they might have seen Mum on the TV and just thought 'Get over it'. People can respond like that to events before their time. I am pretty confident that nobody who was alive then would have been responsible for the destruction. There was universal sympathy, disgust and sentiment that it could have been anyone's child, but happened to be ours.

The only point that still concerns me to this day about these three attacks is that for such a warped mind or minds to have carried out what looks like a needless act of thuggery, there had been some planning. They knew Lesley's birthday, they were fully up to speed on Hindley's bid for freedom in an era when we were still not saturated with news, and they clearly understood exactly where to find Lesley's grave, which I think takes some research. So, there was calculation involved and that is concerning – plus it happened three times. Every year on Lesley's birthday, somebody wanted to make a point. That meant that obsessive compulsive behaviour was floating around in some crackpot's head for longer than three years. They probably pre-occupied their mind for a fourth year too, wondering whether to strike again. For us, this could not go on. We had to take unprecedented action.

It was of course soul-destroying to learn of the attack and then to see it and clear it up. The police aren't bothered about irritations like this. We just had to get on with it. Bar the odd eccentric note through the door, we had never been threatened or besieged at home by stalkers or pro-Hindley campaigners. Most people could see that backing her was an absurd thing to do and even if you privately agreed that after so much time a bid for parole was a genuine option, you didn't go around championing her cause.

So, it was highly concerning that, an individual or several, plotted, researched and then made their move – and they remained out there.

That would end now. As a family, we made the decision to open Lesley's grave, exhume her body and move her to a secret location. We never ever, of course, envisaged such a day. When we said goodbye to her over 30 years before, everybody believed that we literally closed the lid. Now, this was forced upon us and it was too much for me. I couldn't look or attend the new service for her before she was moved. It was tragedy for a second time. The only consolation is that I was told that inside the coffin everything was intact – exactly as we laid her to rest.

In a symbolic gesture, my brother Tommy bought the grave papers for a penny to ensure that Lesley's final resting place would at least stay in the family – and as time would show, we could not know how prophetic that would turn out to be.

Chapter 27

In November 1998, Hindley went to the Court of Appeal who upheld the decision that several previous Home Secretaries had denied her the chance of parole. Hindley was then moved from a top security wing to a medium security prison in Suffolk. She maintained now that Brady had blackmailed her. It *was* unlikely that she was a threat in the outside world, but was that the barometer for freedom – or was it actually the fact that you had deprived someone of their life, so the same fate should be dealt unto you? And for Mum, this rejection was really the door closing for the last time.

It was the end of the line. Hindley's gamble to assist and appear cleansed had got her nowhere. The downgrading of her prison category was as close to any acknowledgement that she might get that she probably was not a risk, but that did not mean she should stop paying. Despite the Longfords of this world, successive governments did not waiver.

Mum could go to her own grave, knowing that she had silenced Hindley for good. Sadly, I describe my Mum's decline as more than a metaphor. Since 1995 when, out of character, she appeared bloated or pregnant at Tommy's daughter, Kimberley's christening, she had been in decline.

She was still determined to attend Hindley's parole hearings in her wheelchair, but the truth was she had done well to survive this long. She had in fact been in steady freefall since before Lesley was taken from us.

When pregnant with Brett in 1960, she developed pneumonia and then TB. After Lesley, she spent her lifetime on tranquilisers and sedatives, without knowledge back then of the consequences. Her daily battle was to survive the light and to subside into the night. In the beginning, that medication was essential – the shaking with anxiety, stress, and uncertainty a constant. That, of course, bred dependency when she may have been able to reduce her intake. The irony is that after the trial their effect began to wear off, so she took more to fight it – consuming amounts way beyond her prescription.

By 1980 and 1982, the inevitable happened. Mum overdosed – intentionally. The tape, the mortuary, the everything – nightmares were meant for sleep, but she was living them. She chose to knock herself out once and for all.

When she had been able to function outside of that zest that came from nowhere to quash Hindley, she could be a liability because of the medication, once crossing near home in a dazed state, only to awake in hospital having been hit by a car, bouncing into the road. On another occasion she came home from work believing she had indigestion after taking Rennies for six months, when in fact that meant seven weeks in hospital for a heart attack. As a result, bronchitis and asthma followed and then further emergency surgery where the doctors discovered cancer of the ovaries. She was told by Wythenshawe Hospital that she had been half an hour from death.

Somehow she was surviving, fighting on when everything else was telling her it was over – and this was 1982. Sometimes, the body just gives up. When she recovered, she attended Withington's psychiatric unit of her own accord. It was her first attempt to lose the pills since she started taking them – the best part of twenty years previously. She knew that time was slipping away then and, whilst her mission continued against Hindley, she had at least attempted to find some quality of life. But, that kind of environment was not for her, so she discharged herself and then hit the pills again. All she wanted was to clear her mind of the appalling memories, but that left her chasing the tablet, which meant she was soon back in care.

An abnormality of the lung followed – and the vagary of that word actually meant a dormant cancer on one side. By 1997, it was confirmed. Mum was terminally ill.

When people talk of their dying wish and they trot it out like a cliché, I have lived and breathed that ethos and know what it truly means. Mum should not have survived until the 1998 ruling on Hindley, but somehow she fought on. I have found an old press article from 1997, which says she has weeks to live. I am not entirely sure that was true, but the fact that she lived on over another year underlines everything you probably sense about the strength of this woman.

Beautifully too as Hindley ran out of legal process – and Heaven only knows at what cost and to whom – Brady turned on her in a furious open letter to the next Home Secretary, who was now Labour's Jack Straw. Individuals who had grown up watching this unfold on the news and had chosen a path in politics now found history caught up with them and Straw had been the latest to condemn Hindley.

The notion that she had been coerced by him set him off and he fired off his missive to Downing Street, referring to her '33 years of duplicity' and a 'Barbara Cartland prose'. He slated her for sacrificing all her 'moral and intellectual credibility and integrity'. What, as though this had just happened in 1998?

If those two were fighting – and openly so – then good. Let them self-destruct. Through all this, we were hanging onto Mum, but it was obvious the end was nigh. She knew it too because when you renew your wedding vows you are trying to make a big statement and on the day of Princess Diana's funeral there was only one family in the UK not watching – Mum and Alan tied the knot again.

It was a gesture of symbolism. This was an attempt at that closure business. She was saying thank you to Alan for all the years. She knew she was on her way even though she lasted so much longer. She was in effect, tidying up the pieces. She was trying to leave everything in an orderly fashion before she left us all.

As the inevitable came, I recalled memories that I didn't really live with in the moment or at the time. I could only admire my tough, campaigning Mum – images counter-balanced by what the narcotics did. But I did somehow recall happy times and I know that she was enjoying life when she travelled – Belgium, a particular and unfashionably sophisticated getaway for her and Alan.

184

I looked at her as a life deprived of sunlight, but out of the darkness emerged a shining example of how the working class underdog should never roll over and succumb to the prejudices of class in the United Kingdom and nothing exemplified this more than the fool, Lord Longford. She was also the most vocal of all the victim's families. I felt that responsibility passing to me on her death, but it was not something I could easily deal with. I recognised that the noise might die down with Mum's passing, but that didn't mean that the heat should fade on Hindley and Brady.

More so Hindley, if I am honest because Brady was Brady and not making any case for his own release. His only interest was his ego and legacy. The truth is that they were aspirations only in his own mind.

None of what either of them said could even come close to my Mum's last words to me as she lay down in the bedroom downstairs.

'When I go to Heaven, I am going to see our lovely Lesley.'

And finally, they were re-united.

Chapter 28

It was 9 February 1999. Mum didn't make the next millennium. That seems fitting that she would not make the dawn of a new era and a physical turning over of the calendar could symbolise leaving events behind. People were looking to the year 2000 for a new start. Equally, she almost had enough fight to see it through bloody-mindedly. Interpret it as you wish.

Actually though, they are just days in an endless sequence of time.

The rock at the centre of our family, that tottered so often in the storm, upholding justice and calling the system to account, stood tall and defiantly so often, and despite the battles and the troubles, you can only remember her as a truly gutsy fighter who dedicated her life to making sure nobody forget nor were they allowed to change their viewpoint because time had passed. Brave enough to converse with Lesley's killers and strong enough to appear on national TV, where the haves thought the have-nots were just trash, she was the battler who had been downed a thousand times and more yet still got up to take another blow. This time she wouldn't rise again.

If I am truthful, I think there was relief that Mum had left us – as much for her as ourselves. With the cancer of the ovaries and all the years of struggle, including the attempted suicides and spells in hospital, it is correct to say that we had notice and it came as no surprise. Tears at the funeral were not shed in the unfairness at a loved one being taken away, but they reflected the sadness of the story from start to finish. Just like with Dad. Nobody needed to say on the news that it was more heartache for a family ripped apart by the events of 1964 and the subsequent discoveries of what happened to others the following year. Mum's had been a life dominated by pain. Every single night she spoke to Lesley and every single morning awoke to medication wearing off, and for many years to another fight. Also, don't forget that before Boxing Day, she was scrapping all the time, trying to get her family into a better home. Lesley's death just meant there would never be an end until now.

Her legacy lives on for others in the *Murder Victims Association,* which she founded in 1985, campaigning for the abolition of parole for child murderers and sex offenders at a time when Hindley in particular was gathering momentum. The year after came the *Life is Life* Campaign. Whilst these movements never benefitted our family, I am sure they did others. I understand that Mum felt she was doing something. It echoed that sentiment she had once expressed that she could at least help other mothers, if not herself.

One of her final public announcements was typical Mum and resonated more than the public haranguing of decision-makers for the greater good. She promised she would haunt Hindley from the grave – a phrase that was classic tabloid soundbite, but which she meant and believed every word of. It showed that her anger and her motivations had not subsided a jot. All the correspondence with Lesley's murderers was not a weakening of the soul. It was a strengthening of resolve that she would see this through, extract mental fragility from them and remain appropriate and admirable from the lofty peaks of the moral high ground.

And now she had risen even above that summit. She genuinely believed that she was being set free by her passing from one world to the next and there she would find Lesley. From above, she could torment Hindley in particular – woman to woman – and this would give her power and strength and moral supremacy that she had sometimes found, but was often struggling for on earth.

We knew too as a family that once again our lives would be invaded. When Mum left us, the best thing to say was nothing. They would all soon find out, so we should savour her memories the first 24 hours or so after her death, before the press beat a path to our door. Then, it would all begin again and the mental torture of Lesley's funeral would re-commence. I was so relatively young then that I did not understand the attention and very public nature of that service. We all understood better the media image, its manipulation and the distance it could now travel. None of us wanted a circus this time.

Once again, on advice of the authorities, we were to have a police escort. Cameramen were sat waiting across the Princes Parkway in Manchester with little discretion, already well aware of Mum's route to the cemetery. To give you some idea of how the experiences of one generation transcended upon another, the knock-on effect manifested itself once more as Brett, who had been too young to attend Lesley's funeral, but felt that he had lived every moment of it since, stormed across the highway and ripped out the film from the photographers cameras, tearing that kit from their hands and throwing them to the ground. It did not stop several hiding behind bushes in the cemetery still clicking away. There was never peace or boundaries of decorum. They could try to take the pictures quietly, but the fact is they had crossed the line by entering the graveyard and we knew they were there.

Some of the shots survived and we have seen them since. Long lens photography probably tells you all you need to know about the level of intrusion that they thought was appropriate. Some of the media were courteous and played by the rules. Lurking in the shadows was disrespectful.

Also, my own daughter was not there. I cannot say that Mum's death was directly responsible for her condition, but Charlene was in the midst of a breakdown and attending the funeral was an unnecessary step that would send her further into a downward spiral. But that is why I make the point that Boxing Day 1964 cuts into the DNA of people who weren't there and didn't deserve this pain, but their loyalty, their genetics, their being party to family conversations and walls of photographs, together with their shared love of siblings, off-spring and parents within our unit mean that there is a massive psychological transference to the next generation that burdens them too. Whether it be accusations of desecration or my own lack of expression and emotion, she too went over the edge and the cycle repeated itself.

It was obviously distressing to watch and mental health was not discussed much then, other than in terms of people being 'nutcases'. I could offer little except support. She needed professional help. Ian Brady was living in comfort in a psychiatric hospital. By his actions, he had condemned my own daughter to the same. And he had all the help he wanted, if he genuinely needed it. That was the irony and that was the injustice. His actions cut through to a second generation who were unable to get the support he could have in bundles.

I have no doubt that the difficulty of being born *into* this family was at the source of her breakdown. I stress *into* because the sadness of my daughter's suffering is that it was not triggered by events in her own lifetime. As you go through life, you never know when you come to a crossroads, where your path would have changed if you had gone another way, but these are events cast in front of people who should not have been held back from birth. There is, at least a choice. You can, for example, choose a career in the army and then suffer from PTSD. As awful as that outcome is, there was an option not to take that route.

Charlene's destiny was pre-determined. She was born into a family who would never recover, with a Dad who carried a lifetime of guilt and a muted emotion – let alone the claustrophobia she felt by being the first girl just six or so years after Lesley's death. Her life had a permanent cloud over it. She was both wanted and unwanted – but consistently was the comparison. And in the years when she passed Lesley's age, she was forever the girl whom Lesley might have been. That is how others saw her, but also whom she was dragged into as Mum spared no details in her relentless recounting of what had happened and what we had learned since.

Even Brett, my son, Alan and Brett's daughter, Melissa often said that they had got it lucky because Mum just bombarded her.

I am sure Mum was offloading to a shadow of Lesley inside Charlene – as if it was a sign of love and affection that she felt she could only confide in – dare I say it – a replacement Lesley, or if it was an act of medicine-inspired malice that off-loading made her a bitter target. They had a love-hate relationship, so it was probably both. She felt this proximity because of Lesley that enabled her to express it all, but then withdrawing because Charlene was not Lesley, meant that she fell under her wrath too – hence the grave desecration accusation. That summed up how far we could get as a family emotionally – only so far.

She often saw hostility – from press articles and the toughness with which Mum fought back, to playground whispers and inter-family squabbles. My separation in my first marriage threw away the only attempt at stability she knew and then of course, she was on all sides as a war of words inevitability ensued with my Mum slating Charlene's Mum and vice-versa. From the age of thirteen, she was on and off anti-depressants.

So, Charlene was not well enough to attend and, despite this background, it has eaten her every day since. It also represented a distancing between herself and Mum's Alan, and I understand now that for some time she had bottled up frustrations about their relationship which had begun to consume her at a ferocious rate and in time might have served as a marker for events to come.

Mum was buried a week after her death. Within what seemed no time at all, Alan had done a piece in the *Manchester Evening News* on 'Living without Ann' and this tipped Charlene over – furious that he could even comment so soon after her death, but also livid at one small detail and still angry from the fact that Alan had told the Downey side of the family not to come to the funeral. The article referred to Alan as Lesley Ann's father – sloppy journalism a generation on, possibly written by somebody who hadn't lived through the story. She called the offices of the paper, screaming at them. The erasing of my Dad and her Granddad from the family

190

history and, of course, the story, was an injustice that Charlene would not let pass uncorrected. It was a lazy piece of work, but one which caused so much hurt. So often over the years, we had witnessed so many little details, flakey in their accuracy. It remains upsetting and disrespectful and on the strength this article – but with a nod and a wink to other events within the family – almost instantly the dynamics of our relationship with Alan changed.

I was not about to carry on Mum's campaigning, though I made a promise to myself that I would speak out now if I had to. Alan's mobility was limited too – Mum was the real energy behind seeing off several Home Secretaries. But that chapter was closed. Charlene never spoke to Alan again, as though she had been waiting for Mum to die to get something out of her system.

She rarely spoke to Brett either, which I know she regrets. His silence about his own mental health issues had frustrated her since the day she had gone into see Mum years before in hospital and was casually looking down the patients' lists only to find his name in an adjacent ward at the same time as Mum – something nobody else in the family was aware of. He too, had paid a heavy price in his mind for what had really gone on outside of his time. Mum loved him, but couldn't love him. He cried out for her love. The tears fell on deaf ears.

By the 5 March 1999 – so within a few weeks of Mum dying, Charlene struck a severe blow. She changed her name from West to Downey. She had never been a Downey. She was cutting Alan West out of her life and heading back to roots she felt deprived of. It hadn't been a spontaneous decision in that it had been brewing, but it was an instant reaction at a time of high stress and extreme anxious energy. It was not something she would have done when Mum was alive.

She had been very bitter about one particular injustice – that Lesley's grave had borne the words 'daughter of Ann and Terry', but when we had been forced to move Les, it now read as 'daughter of Ann and Alan'.

She was right that this was wrong.

I don't know if this was the power Mum could hold over you that then set Charlene free in her death. She was a formidable individual and you could still feel her presence after she was gone. Charlene was much closer to her than I ever was, but there was always that wall that went back up because she was not Lesley.

Now, she was tearing it down and running through it.

Chapter 29

In September 1999, Ian Brady went on hunger strike. Who really cared? His argument was that he wanted to be transferred to another hospital where he would be allowed to starve himself to death. At Ashworth he was being force-fed. The hunger strike lasted 14 years – except it didn't because it was a charade. Brady living off toast and soup, a tribunal heard years later.

Meanwhile under the House of Lords Reform, Lord Longford was created a life peer and the eccentricities of the British political system meant that he was still considered fit to operate at the age of 93.

Myra Hindley had her final appeal thrown out against a life sentence at the turn of the millennium. Longford, in all his sanity was still banging that drum that she was a changed woman – as they both had done since the late Sixties. Her crimes resonated sufficiently with successive Home Secretaries that the passage of time or the colour of their politics did *not* cause any of them to waver. Life, for once, did look as though it meant life.

By 2001, Brady – the mental health patient in a psychiatric ward – released a book *The Gates of Janus* in which he analysed serial murder and serial killers. I have not checked its Amazon ranking, but Heaven only knows what the meetings were like with the publisher and its co-writer.

These were sideshows – stuff you read about and gazed to the stars at how you got dragged into this crazy world of polarising people and why it was still going on. Would it ever end?

No.

Tragedy was to strike again a couple of years later.

Alan West was in hospital having a hip operation. I was house-sitting on Princess Road, Manchester. But on 30 December 2001, I received a call from him just before I left, asking me to make my way in to see him and if I could pick up his girlfriend.

This was the first I had heard about her and was somewhat taken aback. A girlfriend? He had the right, of course, but none of us knew. I never liked to upset anyone, so I duly obliged only for the car to break down and for Charlene's husband to come and jump start the vehicle.

Caz Telfer had just walked into our lives.

At hospital, Tommy had been visiting Alan with his kids and Tommy had offered to look after the property in Fallowfield, Manchester, so I could spend some time with Linda. As I was leaving, Alan asked me if I could drop Telfer by the house so she could pick up some car keys and I ended up going in to see the kids.

A little later, I was overcome by a funny feeling – one I did not have on the Boxing Day I didn't go to the fair, but as though I had been given a second chance to intervene. *If only* I could spot the signs this time. Linda called the house to see if Telfer had actually left, only to be told 'no' and that she had started drinking. Tommy decided to call it a night and hit the sack. The next thing – all the smoke alarms are going off and he is rushing downstairs to see that Telfer had set fire to the curtains.

An extraordinary chain of events.

He did his best to put them out, but the fire brigade were already on the way. One of Tommy's kids, Stuart, had earlier asked to go home because he felt a bit frightened, but Tommy assured them they would all be fine. Except that Telfer had knocked the battery out of the smoke alarm this time and set fire to the house once more. This time Tommy ran down the stairs with both Kimberley and Stuart in his arms, managing only to get Stuart to safety, who now had a fractured rib after Tommy banged into Stuart's side on the bannister. Kimberley had seen the flames in the bay window and, terrified, had retreated back up the stairs.

Tommy had no chance but to go back after her and found himself trapped on all sides. He never stood a chance.

194

He didn't make it back out as Caz Telfer wailed meekly outside the window for help, when in fact that was not her intention, sending the fireman to the back of the house when Tommy and Kimberley were in the front bedroom.

By the time they got in it was now the early hours of New Years Eve and Tommy was slumped over Kimberley trying to protect her. Kimberley died at the scene. She didn't even make the Royal Infirmary Hospital. Stuart was admitted for his rib and smoke inhalation. By the time we saw him on the ward, it brought tears to my eyes – the young lad, lost and bewildered, and on oxygen with the pale look of a ghost or a Zombie, but all the time still with the stains of soot covering his body. Saying goodbye that night became more heart-breaking than coming to terms with the injuries. Once you accept the physical damage to your body, you are stuck with it and you know that time can heal and the medical staff can work miracles. We had spent enough time in hospital to know that Stuart would be fine in the long run. But what it does to the mind and the heart is more crippling. Every time someone left a lad like Stuart, you plunge them back into a world of loneliness, doubt and emptiness. In the end, telling him we loved him was too much. He now had lost his Dad and sister and only on the days ahead would he start to realise the impact.

I had been oblivious to everything that was going on until Tommy's step-daughter, Lisa, called me screaming down the phone. My gut feeling, from the very little I knew, was that there was something not right about Telfer, but I hadn't said anything as I did not want to rock the boat. I had also barely met her. Nobody could have imagined it would come to this. Another New Year – in the year we lost Mum – and now another tragedy. Another tragedy and another cycle beginning, its likely effects would take root and embed themselves in our family for at least another two generations – if our previous experiences were the benchmark by which to judge. Another moment in time which I could have prevented.

Early the next morning Linda took charge, calling Charlene.

'Tommy's dead,' she screamed to my barely awake daughter, confused by the darkness at that time of year.

'What you talking about?' she replied.

And Linda was making very little sense either.

'Granddad's girlfriend. Your Dad wants you here now,' she jumped forward in her explanation.

Shocked and nervously not really retaining what had been said, she made her way over in the snow, listening to a Paul Weller song on the car CD that had automatically started playing – a clear sign that the panic in Linda's voice hadn't got it through clearly enough that Tommy was gone.

She understood enough to come, but her demeanour defied the physical reactions of somebody in shock and grieving. Perhaps, it was delayed reaction and she did hear clearly.

When she got out of the car, she came up the drive, not taking any of it in and asking, 'What do you mean, Tommy is dead?' as though she thought it was a sick joke.

You don't obviously mess about with things like this, particularly when as a family you have been here before. I have no idea what she must have been thinking in the car coming over – as if waking up or the difficult cold weather had numbed her now. She had caught enough of what Linda had said to know that it was serious enough to come, but her tone was very much as though it couldn't be true. Now, a trance like stare came over her face – almost an out of body experience taking her into autopilot. I had seen this all before. Now, I saw it in my own daughter.

I grabbed her and ushered her in the house. Too much of our grief had been on doorsteps.

'What do you mean, Tommy's dead?' she said.

'And Kimberley,' was all I could reply.

I blurted it out without any way of knowing how to. The only previous experience I had was when the two officers came to the house and asked Mum to identify Lesley, but their language let slip they knew it was our Les when either their orders or attempt at discretion had been signposting doubt.

196

This was different. There is no rehearsal for moments like this. If Lesley's abduction at the fair was an extreme act for which we had no immediate resolution, in that we waited months for both misinformation and accurate detail, then despite being my brother, and his little seven-year-old perishing, this was so different because we had information immediately.

I had not, for example, known that Alan had a girlfriend, despite staying in touch with him as much as I did when Mum was alive. I don't know if she was a secret out of embarrassment, the circumstances in which they met, or if Alan knew there was something odd about her. But Tommy must have known because his step-daughter, Lisa, was always taking meals around for Alan as they lived so close. Telfer had been there. How could I have not known? How could Tommy be aware, yet I wasn't? It was not that I was being naïve. She was being kept a secret.

Caz Telfer *was* indeed known to us. This time our tears were short-lived, not at a lack of grief, but because anger and mistrust replaced them. On one of the many occasions that Mum was in hospital, Caz Telfer's Aunt was also in at the same time. That is where Mum met Telfer and the process of befriending Alan West had begun.

Chapter 30

It cut the family in two once more. I was devastated. After I split from Lorraine, Tommy was of great comfort to me, popping round all the time and, together, we went to Manchester United. I could not have got through without him.

Charlene would spend much of the next few weeks driving down the street of the house, hallucinating that she had seen Tommy. The repetition of the route – making it her routine – and the constant mis-sightings were classic grief. Now, what had happened to me was happening to my daughter. The video was playing, but the freeze-frame would not let you go back past a certain point. I had suffered with this for years and had reason to do so because I didn't take Lesley to the fair. Charlene was not in any way responsible, but she could see history repeating itself and it did not matter that she was born after Lesley's death. She had spent so much of her life in the slipstream of everybody else's emotional fallout and now she was experiencing it in real time too. She changed forever at that moment, refusing to come to terms with it for at least five years and that of course had consequence for all around her.

I could see in her my failings – how hard I was to penetrate, bearing that glazed look all the time. Now, that was her and she bore an anger that she had never really expressed before, fighting back like her Nana and sticking up for herself for the first time when she was taking on the hardships of life. Whereas I had withdrawn and had been unable to communicate in my first marriage, she went the other way, and in every cause, she saw an argument. She was not going to lose again in life – her Uncle Tommy and her had been thick as thieves – everybody said she was the female version of him. He was her big brother, her second father, godmother to his daughter, and one of the few who had stood up to Mum when she was having one of her less good days against Charlene. From that, I think, she found her new-found voice in Tommy's absence. It also, of course, bore an uncanny resemblance to Mum.

So, in amongst this latest tragedy, she had lost part of her spirit. Ahead for her lay the double whammy of funeral and then the legal process. Her emotional energy and mental welfare were about to be zapped. We had all been here before.

The worst possible start to the year. To bury Tommy and Kimberley.

Chaz went to their house early. Their bodies were already there – a chance to reflect in the private calm. My daughter is one of those people who always picks up on a sign. At Lesley's funeral, those two dogs had run through the house and nobody knew what it meant.

Chaz had this instinct about two songs that were to be played during the ceremony. One was Handbags and Gladrags by The Stereophonics. Suddenly it came on the radio in the morning. She began hovering nervously by the speaker, like the old days when you were desperately trying to make out the football results late at night on crackly medium wave. Everyone else was just getting ready.

The next thing – Angels by Shaggy is playing. These were both unusual funeral choices, but they were their songs. And now they were playing back to back on the radio. I don't know what it meant, but I know it was a sign. What does that sign mean? Who knows, because if there is a God, he is surely too busy to be programming local radio stations? It was an incredible tonic, though and somehow made her feel so much better. The radio had convinced her that it was all going to be OK, when of course, that really was not true. Sometimes, there are other forces at work.

Oddly, it did not end there. For Kimberley's previous birthday, she had spent a significant sum of money on some Barbie books for her. It is the morning of the funeral and the phone rings. The company who sold Chaz the books some time ago have randomly chosen this moment to call. Would she be interested in some other books for Kimberley?

Timing, as they say, is everything.

Charlene stopped her in her tracks and explained the situation that we were about to bury her and could she remove us from their mailing lists, despite it being the only communication since purchase!

These two moments seemed extraordinary in their coincidence.

But from here, we have to suspend our disbelief and pull ourselves together from the randomness of life towards the certainty of death. That meant, in moments, I was faced with both coffins departing through the front garden.

This time, we did have a few moments with the bodies, saying goodbyes over and over again. Flowers just kept coming to the door.

I can't say that I have been here before in a way that makes me hardened to it. In fact, I know I was very distant on the day. A lot of that was because for the first time I could see the reflection. That means that the pain my daughter was experiencing mirrored where I had been all those years ago. Consequently, if I am honest, I was little help to her. I struggled to console her. Every time you did this in tragedy was a new time. Experience didn't fine-tune it for you. For Chaz, it really was new ground and from those signs of hope, she began to wobble, escorted by Tommy's eldest son, Lee, as she struggled to make her way to the cars.

As fate would have it, Chaz was now 'promoted' to the main vehicle. Alan West was due to take a seat there, but claimed to be too unwell to attend, though had asked for the cortege to make its way via his house on Princess Parkway. This really did test all the emotions, despite my loyalty to him.

Again, the media presence was colossal. The public also, out of curiosity or voyeurism, also turned out en masse. On the journey, we settled a little and smiled to ourselves as the procession was led by a lady in top hat and tails lauding out in front. Tommy loved the ladies and he would have loved that.

But these were brief moments. When we entered the church, Tommy's song was playing and that set Charlene off. I was trying to preserve myself for all the emotional strength I needed for the reading I had to do later. It had been on my mind for days and I didn't get through without choking. Tommy had been a very placid character – the opposite of Mum – but the apple of her eye. Somehow, he had won some love that Brett, in particular, just couldn't grasp. I was so far out of my comfort zone, but I knew it was my responsibility to deliver somehow and, somehow, I got through.

As we left the church to Kimberley's song, I was a pallbearer. I am a small man, so the weight was enormous for me. I could only clutch at thin air as the world's media waited one more time. And, if there was a shot they were looking for – well, Winnie Johnson was on the opposite side of the church. I was about to get back in the car when Winnie called me over. I couldn't not go and see her and – as we had all done on so many occasions – appreciated each other's support.

She hugged me intensely, her hands around my face. A moment of spontaneity became tomorrow's front pages.

It was time to go. The worst was over – except we still had to pass a gathering of Kimberley's classmates on the way home. Heart-breaking, for everyone.

We didn't detour via Alan West's home on the way back. Once was enough. At the cemetery, poor Brett didn't even know where to throw the red and white roses. He was blind by now. One thing kept me going throughout. Mum, Lesley, Tommy – and Kimberley were now reunited. Remember, Tommy had bought the papers to the plot, as if somehow, he had received a sign.

And when we had said our goodbyes, the family was facing court again. Telfer was to stand trial on charges of murder, attempted murder and arson. We had to wait another nine months – once again time taken from the family swallowed up in our own grieving and waiting for due process to take its timely course, attempting to keep our jobs, relationships and lives on track whilst also preparing as witnesses.

Most families will go a lifetime without one such public scrutiny. Now, lightning had struck twice. It brought it all back and even though I did not attend at Chester for Brady and Hindley's trial, in an instant the atmosphere returned – that sense of butterflies in the morning, ignorance of court proceedings, the eternal clock ticking with no end in sight and an overwhelming suspicion that a decent barrister would twist anything to reduce the sentence, meant that sickly feeling in my stomach had returned as it had on so many occasions. It was not a case of taking some pills or have a stiff drink, when anxiety kicks in it becomes an unavoidable propelling force.

Plus – there was the press to deal with again too. Interest was high at the time of the fire when it *was* reported that we were the 'Moors Murder family', but in the period before trial, a judge had imposed a media blackout to protect the jury from preconceptions or sympathetic mood swings towards us. That is standard legal fare, but it does little for the family, of course. Journalists knew, but the twelve sitting members of the public couldn't and didn't. The court was inevitably packed. The clues were all there that this was more than arson and attempted murder.

This time, I went every day. I was older and knew that I was the last person left to step up to the plate. I thought I just about did OK in giving evidence. I had tried to go to the house on the night, but was told I couldn't approach it as it was too dangerous. The court had a record of all my calls. They also heard testimony that she had an attention-seeking disorder, was a Moors Murder obsessive and showed no remorse.

My daughter, sat in court watching, told me that she could see I was in distress and was uppity in my answers, clearly undermined by the whole court scenario. It is a horrible experience. Linda just stared at Telfer. Again, eyeballing your tormentors was tough, but a moral victory. After my testimony, I was shattered and we went straight home. I understand my face was screwed up, tight with stress.

But, I was a grown man. Poor little, Stuart, Tommy's son and realistically, the only true witness, was to face the

202

toughest task. Hindsight provokes this reaction, but he was assigned Maggie Oliver as Family Liaison Officer. She later came to prominence through her outstanding perseverance to expose abuse crimes in Rochdale on the outside of Manchester. Clearly, we had been placed in the care of a very skilled operative in a high profile case.

Stuart was supposed to give evidence alone, but I asked Charlene to go and sit with him. The poor lad had already given evidence at the station and that was harrowing enough. He was just ten years old.

Unbelievably, even this was problematic. The video manager, in charge of Stuart, had to jump through hoops to clear Chaz, first confirming that she was a relative and then for some reason only being satisfied that she had passed herself as under 30. Surely, it did not matter if a minor need any moral support. Apparently, it did.

Of course, the graphic evidence of the fire was the worst testimony. There were light-hearted moments too as they could not make eye contact with Stuart unless he was boosted by cushions to meet the level of the camera.

But genuinely, it was horrific with my nephew being asked questions like 'did you see her light the fire?'

It was disgusting and to think that a barrister, an upholder of the law, could put a child through this because he had to defend his client, revolted me in the same way that Brady and Hindley had pleaded not guilty. We were all seething and had to restrain ourselves from reacting. You hoped a jury could see through it all.

Stuart did brilliantly, answering every question, but then afterwards when he wanted a hug from his Mum, Lesley, who was also due to testify, he was told that he couldn't be talking to her for fear of contaminating the evidence. He was ten. That was his Mum. He needed a hug.

It was ridiculous.

But he left court, skipping up the road. He knew that he had done a great job and that doing so had set *him* free. The weight of the world had been removed from his shoulders.

Alan West was due to give evidence, but somehow got a doctor's note that he was unfit and avoided scrutiny, yet miraculously managed to turn up for the sentencing verdict, leaving Charlene fuming. We had tried to understand a sequence of events since, but with Alan being guarded about his relationship with her and Tommy, who clearly knew more, gone, there was little we could say except recall the events of the night and this then provoked Telfer's barrister into an attempt to turn it back on us.

Telfer was now peddling the line that there was no relationship between the two of them, but that Alan wanted more. There was a 30 year age gap between the two of them. This left me seething for the first time because when I had gone to clear the house after the fire, I had found a picture buried under a carpet of Alan and Telfer with his arm around her. He had the right to move on after Mum, but the smoke and mirrors that were evolving had consequence, as had his choice of woman. I had now lost a sister, a brother and a niece. Others too had left us as a by-product of what had gone on.

Chaz retreated to Lesley's house with Stuart, at which point we received a call from a police officer to say that she hadn't been required to give evidence and that the jury was now considering their verdict. That sounded like a good sign. But it left us nervous. We were relieved, but anxious. It was all just a flashback to what Chester must have been like.

As soon as the jury returned, I knew the verdict. I just knew. I had looked at the fireman too who had sat through it all. They were not hiding from the truth. If I said that I couldn't be happier then that applies contentment. The truth is there was only satisfaction to be had that justice had not been thrown off course.

But still we had to wait.

The judge found her 'not guilty of murder' before considering the other verdicts, *but* waiting six weeks for psychiatric assessments.

By the conclusion of the trial a fortnight after it began the blackout was lifted on naming our family, but by then it had taken its toll.

I know Charlene was so cross to the point that she felt Alan might as well have lit the match himself for introducing her into our world, but the fact that Telfer was not removed after the first fire resonated loudly – sentiments echoed by the Fire Inspector, who gave testimony that the chances of two fires starting in the same house on the same day racked up odds of close to a billion to one. There was no coincidence about any of this, however much a legal team might try to dress it up.

Mr Justice Sachs, passing sentence told her that 'The West family are no strangers to tragedy. You have added to it by your actions in a monstrously cruel way.'

At the start of the trial and not knowing really how courts worked, it felt wrong that the jury were not made aware of our past. She received an eighteen year jail term.

At the conclusion, you can perhaps understand that the twelve members of the public might be more resolute in our favour if they knew our past, though of course it is the judge who determines how long she spends inside. The fact of the matter remains that our past was relevant, because she was in fact a Moors stalker.

You will note earlier that I also referred to her as Caron Foley/Caz Telfer. She was clearly running from herself and her own mental health problems and addictions. Sadly, she stormed into our lives with disastrous effects.

I blame myself again for not having enough nous to follow through my gut feeling that prompted Linda to call before the fire. I am frustrated that Alan allowed this woman into our lives, having hid her and trying to protect her.

Our Lesley's death was needless, nasty, cruel and avoidable. This was needless, nasty, cruel and avoidable too – but on a different level. He had allowed this woman to enter our lives. That facilitated our Tommy and Kimberley leaving our's.

She had sent a devastating hurricane into our lives. And Alan had been blown along by it. I can understand if he felt empty and meaningless, indeed flattered, but also free after Mum's passing away.

There is no escaping the truth, though. His involvement with Caz Telfer cost us again.

There was no bringing Tommy or Kimberley back.

Yet, when I think back to that night, one thing stands out and proof that people say the oddest things at the strangest times – so random they are either blatant nonsense or close to what they are actually thinking. Like David Smith saying how like Lesley I was, which echoed throughout the family for years, to the point that nobody could remember much else that he had said, Alan West began to put distance between himself and the family.

Not just through his actions and the path of destruction that Telfer wove with devastating consequences, but also with his words.

All I can remember him saying on that night I lost my brother and his little girl was one thing – 'how is my dog?'

Chapter 31

You can spend large parts of your life looking over your shoulder, thinking what is next. You start to question how you are lucky enough to still be here, but sufficiently unlucky that all these things had happened to one family. The truth is that Caz Telfer was a direct result of The Moors Murders. One tragedy was bad enough. The second was totally avoidable.

Looking back and stepping aside, I can honestly say that I have learned two things. Beyond the acts themselves, I could not have any sense that this set of circumstances would ruin the next generation's life too.

Charlene has been deeply tormented by Tommy's death. She was already carrying the burden of Mum. It clearly affects the way people who lived through it interact with the next generation.

The second is the amount of time and energy that is given up to witness statements, police visits, reporting, misinformation and waiting for court. Not only have we lost cherished lives. We have wasted so much time in between coming to terms and waiting for the authorities' next move.

These were our lives. Some 37 years had passed from Lesley's death to Tommy's. That is a considerable period of time. It was always one step forward two steps back. A period of calmness and coming to terms would be disturbed by illness in the family or ill-timed news reports and the constant rumbling in the background that never went away.

Hindley's determination to pursue parole meant that even in the 1980s when you would hope we might find some peace, we were still fighting and trying to muffle that whole noise – and that is what it was. You would turn on the television and ther would be a story and you would mutter something back at the box and walk away, but then, of course, human instinct and the need to protect the family meant you really ought to keep on top of the constant drip feed, because one thing was certain – somebody else at work, at football or at school, someone would be likely to be whispering about it. You had to educate the kids without overloading them.

We were living parallel lives, trying to cope and find a peace, but all the time at the mercy of events in the outside world. When you learned that Hindley had been knocked back for parole, your faith was re-instated and you muttered under your breath, 'bloody right too', whilst remembering what Mum had said what she would do if she ever got out and therefore questioning what you might now do as the head of the family. But then when you discovered that Hindley would not let up and was heading to Strasbourg to the European Court of Human Rights, you knew that once again this was ticking in the background and that it might be another two years ahead.

I realise that lawyers get paid handsomely, but I have struggled over the decades to see how a lack of moral fibre manifests itself that somehow they could find reasonable legal argument to defend the woman. Perhaps they become immune to emotion and money talks – or maybe they are drawn to the notoriety of the case and want to make a name for themselves.

In May 2002, a test case concerning Dennis Stafford from Newcastle, jailed for his role in gangland murders that inspired the Michael Caine film, *Get Carter*, won his appeal against the British Home Secretary, David Blunkett. Stafford had served twelve years, but was released, only to later be sent back to prison. The argument concerned a Home Secretary's right to set or increase a tariff in relation to a prison term.

On Jack Straw's watch, Hindley had been unsuccessful – the tariff of a life sentence *was* deemed lawful and life did mean life. But that decision came six months before the Human Rights Act came into effect in September 2000. Hindley's lawyers had quietly lodged an appeal at Strasbourg, citing Article 3 (inhuman or degrading treatment or punishment) and Article 6 (the right to a fair trial) and Article 7 (the right not to have a heavier penalty imposed retrospectively).

I am assuming the taxpayer was funding this. It did your nerves no good whatsoever. You got sucked in, thinking there was a groundswell of momentum and that at some point, somebody was going to give in, and buoyed by the Stafford case, we now had a new set of legal parameters, whereby a European Court and not our own could overturn British law and set Hindley free.

I am sure you understand that when I say one step forward two steps back it really has been a life when you feel someone is snapping at your heels. Just when you put some daylight between all *this* and everything else, the everything else catches you up again.

Shockingly by November 2002, it looked as though Hindley and many others would be released. The law lords were about to conclude that it was not the right of the Home Secretary to set minimum sentences. Blunkett is said to have contacted Greater Manchester Police to find new charges to be brought against her, including the murders of Keith Bennett and Pauline Reade in a bid to keep her inside, but was advised against by government lawyers and it is understood that plans were well afoot to give Hindley a new identity on her release. It had got that far. Our suspicion across various governments that one would eventually cave in looked like it was becoming a reality – except this was Britain in a new Europe, where other decision makers were involved.

My stomach was rumbling, twisting in knots. Mum, helpless from beyond the grave, would have been seething. I am not confrontational by nature, but was at a loss what to do. Mum would have found Hindley, whatever she now looked like or wherever she might be living. It would have probably given her strength to carry on a few more years. I really never thought it would come to this. Despite the paranoia every time Hindley filed an appeal and that sense that she had momentum, *I* still believed that in Britain life meant life and I had never prepared myself for the reality that she might walk free. My worst nightmare was about to happen.

Then, on 15 November it was over. Years of uncertainty and speculation came to an end. Hindley took the matter out of our hands. She was dead.

At 60 and ten days before the Home Secretary's power to set minimum sentences was stripped, she succumbed to bronchial pneumonia, caused by heart failure. She was a heavy smoker who had previously suffered an angina and a brain aneurysm. I felt justice had been done – that somehow she hadn't just run out of time, but that somebody had called time on her, so close to the law lords' ruling.

I sunk to my knees in relief, tears swelling that it was finished. Just Brady to go now.

I wanted to dance for England – for all the years of pain, for Mum and for Lesley. Her cockiness and mock angelic pose of this reformed character had lost in the end. For once, something had gone right for the family. When you are not surrounded by luck, you give up believing that anything will ever go your way and her death was neither here nor there as a physical act. She had been killing herself with her tobacco as her age suggests. Her death filled me with joy for two reasons.

It brought an end to the noise – the funding of her legal fight was over, and so were the arguments. She wouldn't have considered for one moment the effect of mentally chipping away at us all those years. I breathed a little easier that night.

Secondly, the timing of it was beautiful. There is no element of having the last laugh, because this is a dark and grim story, but to know that she had spent all that time campaigning and it looked finally as though she was getting somewhere to me, meant that Mum was vindicated and in giving her entire life to the cause had ultimately won. So close to the law lords' verdict, it was a sweet moment to know that she died not knowing.

Her funeral was attended by less than a dozen people, and none of her relatives. The press was there en masse, of course. It felt good that the lens was now on her. It is rumoured that most of the local undertakers refused to handle her cremation. I can't imagine who the warped few in attendance were but, given there were no family members, I struggle to see why and how. I believe one of them may have been her ex-partner, Patricia Cairns, who then chose to scatter her ashes less than 20 miles from Saddleworth Moor, despite Hindley seeing out her days in Suffolk. She had also requested her barrister be present – her legal representative just happened to be married to a granddaughter of Lord Longford.

She knew she was dying, but with, what I can imagine was as, one last act of defiance, had chosen to see through her legal fight. They had even given her nicotine patches at a cost of £20 a week in a bid to stop her smoking. I know that is probably some standard procedure with all inmates, but I can't help but wonder what were they thinking with this particular inmate?

Reverend Michael Teader would visit her every Wednesday. He was one of the last to see her in her final confession and it is he alone who can recount Hindley's state of mind as she died, claiming that she was deeply remorseful for the murders. Remorse only goes so far though when you won't give answers to the family of Pauline Reade and Keith Bennett.

She was given the last rites, believing she would go to Heaven. I read that Brady had watched without emotion as news broke on the television.

I doubted the former and believed the latter. Of course, my thoughts turned to him. When it was his turn, then we would be done.

As ever, things were never going to be that straightforward.

Chapter 32

You cannot *live* your life waiting for Brady to die and then thinking it will all be over. You can *wait* for the pleasure, but you have to crack on and deal with all the mental health issues that this has inflicted on the family and then everybody else whom you have befriended by association – notably the other families.

So, still there was noise in the background. Hindley's passing meant there was just Brady to deal with, but it also underlined that he had the audience all to himself. Where previously, she would furrow this lone tunnel to freedom and he would rebuke her and contradict her statements (often playing catch-up), now he could remain unchallenged in his outpourings. Hindley was dead, as was her sister. Brady could continue with his mind games alone.

Plus, he did not want for the benefits of the system and, as with Hindley, somebody smart was looking at every loophole to make someone else bear the cost. Many people have bemoaned that a prisoner's life is actually quite cushy, with mobile phones and Sky TV. Most fair-minded thinking people I know believe that these individuals should do their time in the most minimalistic environment available and when you have been involved in a story like this, you become drawn to others, so when you watch the BBC's *Crimewatch* or ITV's *The Tonight Programme* and you see criminals with miscarriages of justice overturned, it becomes a comparison and you form a kind of league table of whose crime is worse.

The injustice and mental torture remain because you then weigh up your Mum's fight through red tape to get a better council house against a system providing Brady and Hindley with lifelines and opportunities to express themselves. They have the means to legally challenge that just piles on a mountain of injustice on top of everything you have already experienced. Nobody thinks about that.

Quite clearly, Brady and Hindley are murderers and torturers of children. Intellectually, if you can move past that, you cannot bypass the level of pre-meditation and planning. You really do despair when the system gives them hope …and rights. I think many people would agree that if you deprive someone of a life – or even not that extreme – then fairness should rule that the individual be deprived of the same.

So, with funding, legal aid, and for Hindley, with Lord Longford behind her, how can we calculate that liberties such as day release for a funeral are fair?

But then there is the other side of the coin. Peggy Brady, his real Mum, was dying and David Blunkett granted a 'last meeting' as a 'one-off death-bed wish', under The Mental Health Act. A spokesman for Blunkett said that 'she is not a criminal and does have rights under The Human Rights Act'. Under police guard and that of psychiatric nurses, he was allowed an hour with her – or better perhaps, she was given sixty minutes with him. He gained some sort of freedom, because of her rights. She has to be entitled to that – I believe – but sanctioning it, of course, gives Brady rights too.

What are you supposed to feel when you learn about this? You have compassion for the mother because you are a human being and a parent and a decent person, then you struggle with the fresh air that Brady is allowed to breathe, even if it is for just a moment as he exits the police van to walk to the ward. Although, it was his mother's request, I am sure he smugly revelled in tasting freedom for the first time and, albeit an hour's worth, for his Mum's benefit that was still a clock ticking which had stood still for us and Lesley. There is possibly no right answer.

Whilst there was a nagging fear that the passage of time might mean that successive Home Secretaries might not relate and therefore relent in possibly releasing Hindley (even though on David Blunkett's watch it was out of his hands in that it was European Law), it was not lost on the family that the generation who remembered were still horrified, and even though as a nation we since had lived through the IRA,

Muswell Hill and the Yorkshire Ripper, to name but a few, the majority of people seemed resolute that life meant life, whenever they were born.

You could not know exactly the mentality of incoming police into their profession who were perhaps younger than Lesley would be now or not born when all this happened, but generally, the force kept in touch over a long period of time to inform us when there were key developments that might affect the family and I do respect that.

Yes – often (more so than just time to time) someone would tell us stuff or the Sunday papers might claim an exclusive – coupled with the fact that the Internet gave new oxygen to the Caz Telfers of this world. Its advantage was that it kept Lesley's memory alive, but you could even read transcripts online now of her torture, which would have been buried in national archives previously. The downside was that the village idiot had a voice and yesterday's graffiti on a council wall became today's rant on Facebook. In time, we would discover a fake Twitter account in the name of @LesleyAnnDowney, which the social media platform refused to remove, despite it containing such bile as:

'I can't wait for tomorrow, Keith, is knocking for me and then we're meeting John in the park.'

Another generation had deemed our story irrelevant and worthy of mockery.

And for every diligent officer who dealt with us compassionately, who didn't want to be the glory cop that solved all of the Moors Murders?

I can't criticise any officer for that, but I had seen politicians a plenty and journalists all over the world see their own self-promotion in this tragedy.

So, in 2003 it began again. I think every generation sees an opportunity for that variety of reasons. Legislation gets questioned, technology improves, unspoken stories emerge in drip feed and fresh eyes view the case. So despite the belief that the visits to The Moors when Hindley was 'helping' would be the last, it was not actually the case, because the police launched Operation Maida and once again took to Saddleworth in an attempt to find Keith. This time they had raised their game with a digital approach to photography and American satellites used to detect soil movement. I believe nobody is any doubt that the remaining bodies were there, but they found nothing again. By 2009, detectives were quoted as saying that they would not give Brady the media spotlight of another search and despite donations from the public to renew activity, Keith Bennett remains to this day undiscovered. Those who were alive also left mysteries.

So whilst the Moors largely remained untouched – a barren wasteland of emptiness, geographically and now spiritually for us – the moral and legal landscape were changing all the time.

Hindley, with her challenge in the European Courts had shown that. Prisoners did have rights and the avarice of the legal system and the awareness of its customer always seemed weighted in their favour. The fact is that prisoners all over the place were issuing lawsuits under legislation that the average man in the street did not know about and would probably be aghast to learn existed.

I believe we were now split into two camps – old school like me, where you do the crime and you do the time, waiving all human rights for depriving somebody else of theirs, or the modern era, which was 'wait a minute, prisoners have rights too.'

Now, obviously, if you're talking about, for argument's sake, a British citizen incarcerated on some trumped-up charge in a less democratic part of the world then clearly those prisoners *should* have rights.

Brady and Hindley had been served a fair justice. That justice should prevail.

So, in 2007, Brady wanted a piece of the legal action and sues. The taxpayer picks up the bill. His argument is against his former psychiatrist for breach of confidentiality, who used five of *his* photographs in a book called *The Lost*

Boy. The title is a reference to Keith Bennett, whose grave has not been found.

Brady also dismissed the allegation that he took pictures of Keith and John Kilbride before they died, denying any photos existed. His claim is that his human rights have been breached.

I would say that it would be consistent to assume there were photographs. Brady and Hindley were classic pre-determined serial killers and one of those aspects was documenting their victims. Obviously, we know they made recordings of Lesley in particular and there were hundreds of other photos. I think it is a reasonable assumption. But anyway, even if that were untrue, what loss or damage is there to Brady? Furthermore, even if a medical professional used five photos, they are not a disclosure related to his health and whilst they may technically be Brady's, again – is that actually a breach of confidentiality, in that it does not refer to the mental state of Brady? They are in fact nothing to do with Brady, medically, though they may have been obtained under that guise. They may not have been his to publish, but again, at what loss to Brady?

Some of this argument seems to have arisen from a former Medical Director at Ashworth, who contributed to a book about Hindley with Brady, calling into question his own code of ethics. Brady wanted an injunction against him and Ashworth Hospital, where he was detained. Of course, he sought legal aid to pursue this, which was rejected and then subject to appeal!

Wherever you stand on the prisoners have human rights argument, is it not extraordinary that all of a sudden a serial killer, a torturer, and a child abductor who refused to lead the police to Keith Bennett's grave, suddenly was shouting about a code of ethics?

2007 seems to be a year that triggered something in Brady. Maybe he knew time was slipping away, at least for his notoriety, if not his health, just yet. Hindley's bid for freedom before her death also gave *him* the oxygen of publicity. He didn't have much previously, except to counter what she was saying. Now, even though they were on opposing sides of the argument in her later years, his voice seemed muted without a sparring partner, so if he made some proclamation, launched a lawsuit or something was leaked then it looked like he was whimpering out. He had lost his touch. He needed control and part of that meant somebody *to* control. His fear factor and power were on the wane.

From nowhere, and you really do have to question how content like this appears in a newspaper, Brady announced that he would take revenge on Hindley, claiming to have made detailed funeral arrangements, including the disposal of letters sent to him by Hindley, believed to be in code, and with a suggestion that she was in favour of torturing children. Brady claimed that she wrote to him on a weekly basis for six years after they were jailed.

She had admitted that there were letters in 1998, before she really took hold of her bid for freedom and part of that claim was that Brady had forced her to participate in the killings as well as inflicting pain on her and threatening to kill her grandmother, mother and sister.

Previously, Brady had taunted that he would release the letters to the highest bidder. Who on earth other than a National Archive or a Crime Channel would want to purchase them? I can tell you that as somebody who has many pieces of correspondence from him, you feel dirty just holding them. The proximity to his DNA and knowing that his hands had written them leaves a sordid taste in your mouth, but it had been the best way Mum knew to get under his skin.

Distressingly and as an example of their cruelty and obsession with their victims after the event, one of the letters is reported to include Brady urging somebody to throw acid over the face of a four-year-old.

That four-year-old in question was my brother Brett.

Chapter 33

It is now 2 August 2008. My 58th birthday.

I am working on nights at the airport, so have no real body clock and fatigue is the norm.

One of my best and oldest friends, Barry, with whom I spent a lot of time when I got divorced has left us today.

I am devastated. Again. The family had experienced enough tragedy within. Now, I had lost one of the few on the outside who had been allowed in.

I need to lie down and take it all in. Then I must work. I am on autopilot (no pun intended) at Manchester Airport and little time to grieve and plenty to pretend the show must go on. Here we go again.

I am woken by Charlene's voice coming up the stairs. I can hear her and her husband, Mark, coming up the stairs. It is unusual at this time of day, but not out of the question.

She tells me to sit down and steadies me as I come round. I am already lying down, but people say that, don't they?

'Sit down. There is something I need to tell you.'

I repeat. I am already lying down. It is just the language people use.

'Dad, I've got some bad news,' Charlene began.

Brett is dead too.

Wow. Maybe it is easier when all the paths collide on the same day. I don't know. That is a comment I can only make with the passing of time. It is not easier at all. When you stumble into a 'this can't really be happening' dizzy shock, imagine receiving the news for a second time in a day. The well is already dry. You have shed all the tears. You spin some more into a dream sequence, almost recoiling. Tears gone because they came earlier. That emotion is exhausted. The questions start immediately, and denial just like when Charlene came to mine after Tommy and Kimberley's death.

'No, this can't be true?' replaces the acceptance and sadness of Barry's death. You want to fight it, contest it. You get into that 'I need to see for myself' attitude because this cannot happen twice on the same day. You refuse to believe it and then you want proof. The fact that I was barely awake meant that comparing this to a dream sequence is not a cliché. It is the truth. Sound is in delay. You hear what Charlene is saying but your reaction comes later. I need answers, unaware that nobody has them yet. I am reeling. Both my brothers are gone. It is just me now. Why was I lucky enough to survive – or unlucky enough to pick up the pieces?

Charlene took me downstairs. I am struggling to process it. For some reason I call Alan West, even though there was distance between us now. I did not see him much after Tommy's death. Occasionally, Linda would make a meal up and I would take it round and sometimes he would ring. Charlene was constantly on at me for still being in touch with him, but I had promised Mum I would look after him. She would counter by saying that Tommy made the same vow and look what happened to him. She would have let Alan rot. I held that sense of duty. Perhaps she had a point that time was up on that commitment. Caz Telfer really should not have entered our world. I took a lot of stick for still being in touch, but I am loyal and non-confrontational. He simply thanked me for letting him know. I didn't ask him how his dog was.

I don't remember much else of the conversation or anything that was said. I am starting to understand that there is no 'one size fits all' for grief. Lesley and Tommy were both tragedies, but are not comparable. Barry and Brett were not the same. Grief is sadness and anger and regret. It comes with uncertainty of what actually happened in the final moments and longing that you could have changed it, together with concern that there was no suffering in the end. There undoubtedly was for at least Lesley and Tommy. These emotions come together, and on their own. One hour tears, the next wanting to punch the wall, later demanding immediate answers that are not available yet.

The process begins again. Two funerals ahead. Undoubted questions and inquests. Barry's time may have been up, but there is no way Brett's was. So many more questions once more: could anyone have done anything to help him? Why had I not gone round to see him more as Barry had done with me when my first marriage broke down?

Brett and I did not talk a lot. He was often unwell, but I know how much people like Barry had helped me and I am gutted at his loss.

My daughter, Charlene, will tell you that when she got the call, her husband Mark, who is obviously not genetically related to any of this, but might as well have it tattooed on his skull the amount he has had to pick up, simply sighed and said 'What next?' What next had become who next?

People do die. Brett had problems. One of my oldest friends was cracking on. But all on the same day – forgive me for wondering what I had done to deserve this.

Now the familiar scenario of not what or who, but why started. One of Brett's daughters began the process of contacting everyone and said that she had gone round to his flat where he lived, estranged from his wife, and found him dead on the sofa. Blood was exiting his nose. All the times that you say 'I will just go round and check on (someone)', but you never prepare yourself for a problem. It is a peace of mind visit where you go just actually for your own good not theirs. Then, suddenly there really is a problem. And it is too late. The words are futile. As are the actions. Because you didn't go on that one occasion.

The inquest was kept from us. Brett and his wife, Marion, were very private. There were very few people at his funeral. We had to rely on her verdict as the truth. Brett had an enlarged liver. It was twice the size of what it should have been. Over the years, most of his medical struggles had remained within their four walls. I have to accept this because I have nothing else to go on. I struggle slightly that this condition only comes to light at his death, given how much time he had spent on hospital wards. I have to accept this.

Something did not ring true. There had been a moment in the family beyond the fire where Alan West's integrity had been questioned. It had caused major divisions and Brett was very much believing of Alan.

The week before he died, he had rung Linda and asked her to pass a message on to Charlene, apologising for his stance and that he had now come round to a different truth. It was one of the moments that you look back on as coincidence or defining. Was my brother aware of his condition and getting his affairs in order, tying up loose ends, in effect saying goodbye – or is it one of those things? Linda is convinced that he took his own life. Charlene is of the same opinion. I tend to think that whatever the truth, life was taken from him long before it should have ended. From the physical discomfort of being blinded in one eye in the army in Germany to the mental strain of growing up into this and, if I am honest, the absence of parents in his life, he never really was given the best chance to make a shot at things.

It sounds melancholic, but he is a victim too.

I hope you can see that we do not court grief, so bemoaning its arrival in our life is not a hard luck story, but it is *the* story. This is my account of what happened and I am recounting it as a sequence of events, rather than courting sympathy.

There was one overwhelming uncanny echo after Brett's death.

Every week, I would go to the grave, pay my respects and leave flowers or some acknowledgement that I had been. Every week it was tampered with. This time there were no pro-Hindley messages daubed all over the grave. Brett's memorial was private and not part of the spectacle associated with The Moors Murders. Nobody was looking to target his burial, nor was his death public knowledge.

That left me with one conclusion – Mum's nous about Charlene tampering with Lesley Anne's grave was the right thinking, but the wrong person. But, for reasons I cannot understand, somebody was aiming their anger at me and that person was definitely within the family.

Chapter 34

It is now 2010. Brett has been gone two years, Tommy nine, Mum eleven and Lesley Ann 46. That is a massive measurement of time. Each of these seem like yesterday and every year barely a month would pass without a significant date from a birthday to the anniversary of a death rearing its head on the calendar. Whilst we were used to it, there were too many. I would often sit in my chair in silence and say little – my walls adorned with pictures and incomplete memories.

Occasionally, I would go to the loft and bring down some cuttings or some pictures, but it was a long climb up there and a painful afternoon's viewing. It would be normally for someone else's benefit – all of the children and grandchildren would ask in turn at some point and you had to manage how you dealt with it, without overloading as Mum had done to Charlene, avoiding scarring them that bad people were out there, when actually they were probably relatively safe, and trying to communicate all this whilst dealing with your own emotions, or lack of them. It was difficult to express too just how much bad luck we had experienced and to convey that there couldn't be any more ahead. The loft, therefore, remained a sacred place and was visited with caution.

It was easy to find a nice picture from the albums and get nostalgic about how happy Lesley was, and for a moment everyone could feel a calm comfort in her beauty and filled with joy knowing that the camera didn't lie. Pictures of her at church or when she got her sewing machine kit for Christmas tell one half of the story and while you are concentrating on that image and those around say how lovely she looked, you are of course sucked in and agree.

Then with simultaneous timing you put that box away and when you shut its lid, you really close the story and that means that the photos going back inside the box remove the temporary joy and that moment where you brought Lesley back is gone again and you are jolted back to reality.

Silence would normally follow. I would be lost in my own thoughts. Someone would take the box away and say 'let's put these away now', and the short term high of holding the picture, making her real and seeing her dancing before your eyes came crashing back down when you realise that that was then and this is now and in real time, you are probably exceeding your own expectations too.

I had buried my sister and two brothers – and a few others too. You do look around and wonder why it is that you are still here. I had good support, without question, and a lot of understanding from Linda. My own children could see from an early age that this family had become an extraordinary family for all the wrong reasons. When she was free of her own stress, Charlene's breakdown and desire to adopt or foster children definitely helped her understanding of me and that meant that when she was older and well, I did not have to burden her because she just *knew* and understood and that was a mighty relief to me.

By 2010, I worked out that there were probably not many scenarios left in this story. Firstly, there was a wildcard of fate and who could not be on their guard against another Telfer? Secondly, we would lose Alan at some point and finally the man with all the answers – Ian Brady – would die. The latter would undoubtedly provoke chaos and a million more stories, but would be as close as I could get to an ending.

In the interim, whilst Brady was still up to his tricks, there were really only loose ends to sort and I do not mean that in any way to trivialise the location of bodies like Keith, I refer to the slipstream of the whole Moors Murders story.

Enter a woman called Jenny Tighe. She had disappeared from an Oldham children's home in 1964. She was just fourteen.

Before her death, Hindley had reportedly confessed to her murder to fellow prisoner, Linda Calvey. Calvey's lawyer, Giovanni di Stefano, had claimed that he could identify the girl through the initials JT. Newspaper reports then named her.

Greater Manchester Police revealed that Jenny Tighe was alive and her family knew this, but there had been a breakdown in communication between them. They also declared that any link to our story was purely speculative. The lawyer claimed that his office had been in touch with GMP as far back as 2004, but the story had only come to light now after publication on a website.

I found this staggering on many levels. Firstly, we have an actual name of an individual who did go missing at the time. She fitted the type too. Secondly, we seem to have a confession – however reliable – of her abduction.

Where is the line between the two here? Had she been a target, but they had 'failed'? Had she been abducted and fled and never wished to speak of it? Or is it all nonsense? Was there another story?

So that brings a fresh set of questions. There surely must have been a file that had never seen the light of day. In stories like this, many people do come forward with half-stories and sightings and near-misses. Brady and Hindley were calculating and prepared, but they made mistakes too in their planning. If Jenny Tighe was somehow linked to this, I think it is reasonable and understandable to assume she did not want anything but privacy.

If there was no association between her and The Moors then I imagine she felt relief and equally just did not want to get dragged in to any of it. If it is true that she disappeared and there was a family communication problem, then that is a private matter that you would assume they would wish to stay so.

But here she was, close to a half century on, named on the Internet and then forcing a statement from the police? Had they been aware of Jenny all this time (pre 2004) or had they acted in haste as her name got leaked? That is the unfairness of the modern era of social media when yesterday's stories develop a new life of their own in a way that it is not helpful at all.

When I have processed it all, two questions still remain. I also give on this solitary occasion the benefit of the doubt to Hindley who, for whatever end goal (notably parole and freedom) did seem keener towards disclosure, though of course she still had been unable to take the police to bodies on The Moors.

I am not naïve.

I knew her game. The courts would and did decide her fate. If we got any closer to new information as part of her supposed revelation then as far as I was concerned, whatever means was all that mattered.

So where did the name Jenny Tighe come from? What are the unspoken words between her and her jailbird confidante? I think it is acceptable to assume that people in Calvey's position probably enjoy their own moment of fame and like to blab, so is it reasonable to accept that Jenny Tighe was the only name given?

It is impossible to second-guess the context of the conversation. I would struggle to remember somebody's name in that situation if it were mentioned once. Clearly Hindley left a mark on Calvey and she did retain the information. I doubt it was a moment of weakness veering towards confession. I am sure it was calculated to reach a wider audience, but somewhere something is wrong.

Jenny Tighe – the police confirmed – is alive. Hindley is said to have confessed to her murder. Am I wrong to conclude that Jenny Tighe might have been a target or an attempt, but then how did they know names of people who they didn't kill and who weren't reported in the media? Is it incorrect to ask if Hindley therefore got confused and that there is another victim?

I speculate, of course and whilst I have spent my life second-guessing and living with hindsight, this piece of the jigsaw remains a misfit to me.

Chapter 35

I felt confident of one thing - that although this 'lead' went nowhere, despite the element of mystery around it, in that the individual *had* gone missing and that Hindley *did* actually name her, that with Hindley dead, 50% of the game was up.

There would always be people who claimed a near miss. We could never know if there were families out there who always wondered if somehow they were caught up in this mess, and there would always be fantasists who made it their mission to be at its heart – Caz Telfer being one of them.

But unless, a close friend (and who were they?) or a legal representative of Hindley's came forward, her side of events and all double bluffs and red herrings were now concluded. We had to assume so, at least.

Sickeningly, Hindley souvenirs and memorabilia were now available to buy on the Internet.

Brady had always been less forthcoming in his drive. He didn't trade information because he didn't aspire for parole. You could catch him in a rage if he was incensed by a wrong he needed to right. He seemed to watch all the documentaries about himself and befitting the profile of a serial killer, you could picture him pouring over every cutting. He clearly was a clever man – and used his brain to such devastating consequence, with manipulation the key weapon in his armoury, but he frequently wrote to Mum and only really spoke out if he wanted to either toy (as in the searches of the Moors) or if he wanted to contest (what a TV programme may have concluded).

Now, he was mostly silent, because he no longer had Hindley to spar against. Her quest for release failed and she died. All that stuff she was putting out to show she was reformed was also a game against Brady – playing the victim herself, appearing under his trance, coerced into her actions. The man she was once obsessed by was now someone she could see through. By the end of her life, she came across as though she hated him.

That, in effect, gave Brady an open platform for him to speak unopposed. You may well ask yourself that if by 2011 there was actually anything left to say. The answer was clearly yes as we still did not know where other children were buried and if that was the entire number accounted for.

Of course, over the years the police had less and less to tell us and years would pass without hearing from them at all. On Hindley's death they called to advise us first out of courtesy and to prepare for the inevitable intrusion, but their own roles were much broader and digital now and there was almost nobody working in the police who was there at the start of all this. Courtesy remained, but we were the only ones who couldn't move on.

And you may look at this and think that by 2011, we were close to half a century on from what happened. Yet, I can tell you again that time is for history-writers and documentary-makers. It always still remained yesterday.

But, a date had been scheduled for Brady to face a public hearing on his health – a request he had made in August 2010. Justice was very slow moving. I don't know if they dragged it out because it was him or if that was the length of time it took, but it was announced the following year after *he* made the request, making it only the second public mental health hearing ever.

He was arguing against 'the powers of compulsory treatment' and even though the fact that it was going to be public had been revealed, it had in fact been *not* made public for a couple of months after the judge gave the all clear to proceed. Such would be the inevitable scrutiny and security risks as the can of worms opened again, the powers of be sat on it for some time to limit the possible fall-out.

Immediately, as my Mum would have, Winnie Johnson said that she would attend. I know how difficult, but important it was for Mum to have gone to Chester all those years ago and face these monsters, Winnie still had no body, no grave, no burial for Keith Bennett, who had been just twelve at the time. Winnie now had cancer, but stated publicly that she wanted her only chance to get inside his mind and of course, she wanted the opportunity to ask him where Keith was – something that would not be allowed. But I understood totally.

She also declared that it was 'ridiculous' that he was in a mental health unit and that there was nothing wrong with him. When you are inside the victims' families, you are grateful to hear another express this. It hadn't been said often enough that he was playing the system. Brady's motivation was, in part, him now seeking a transfer, so he could be allowed to die in Scotland.

Around this time, his diaries were released too. A man that unstable and in need of mental health care, spent a lot of time writing quite coherent, but disturbing stuff. The tone rings true – his desire to write his own narrative.

So as late as 2011, he began bragging about a minor detail that had been spoken of briefly around the time of his trial – that he had toured Scotland with an arsenal of guns, carrying out contract killings just weeks before Hindley and him were caught. The letters dress it up as a romantic city break, popping into art galleries, then taking somebody out, even advising that inmate of how to spend his time on release, recommending that his fellow prisoner try some museums or head up to Loch Lomond, as they had done prior to being arrested. Re-live Hindley and Brady's magic moments when you get out of here – that was the nonchalant tone.

One correspondence says that at the time he had no intention of being captured alive – hence the two revolvers he carried. Another says that they would not have killed any more children. He tells of how he became friends with the Kray twins and Ronnie Biggs whilst in Durham Prison in the years after his sentencing. This was all posturing for me. Brady had clearly spent significant time talking about us. Hence the letters from some of Britain's most notorious gangsters. How crazy was that?

He wanted to change the perception of himself from a paedophile serial killer to some sort of Ned Kelly gangster. He wanted to play with the big boys. They made movies that often bore a sympathetic nostalgic tone about the Krays and the Ronnie Biggs of this world. He wasn't going to get that write-up, but he was clearly in their company because both wrote to Mum – the Krays even sending flowers to the house, almost laughing at crime and giving that air that they were still controlling it from inside.

He mentions Smith a lot too. That day when he came round and passed me on the stairs is permanently in my head. That knowing turn of phrase he offered without hesitation as to how I looked like Lesley was a guilty choice of language and one split second which has stayed with me a lifetime. He claims that he planned to kill Smith, but spared him because of the family connection – Smith knew too much.

But how was this so? Smith was Brady's Achilles' Heel and he might have got away with it a lot longer without him, but I really do not think you can come down lightly on Smith because he was the whistle-blower. Surely, with Brady unlikely to have shared the intimate details, Smith's involvement must have been greater than he himself claimed.

The story and the stories seemed as alive as they ever were – triggered by news of this public hearing. Years of your life have passed by as you watch your children grow and their own ones too and often little of significance happens, but every few years, the flame is re-ignited and *because* those wheels of justice turn so slowly, we then get wrapped up into another two to three years cycle. Suddenly we were back there again, right in the thick of it and the danger was that once more, people like Winnie thought they might finally get answers. She had all but given up hope in 2010 when a massive fundraising event had raised £3000 to fund a private search for Keith after the police had officially called off the search the previous year. That had been the end of the line.

In June 1964, she waved Keith off from Eston Street in Longsight, just days after his 12th birthday, never to see him again. Now, she could at least bookend her grief by confronting the monster in person.

Chapter 36

A cruel irony:

Winnie passed away on 18 August 2012. She never found out or got to eyeball her son's killer. She was buried with Keith's glasses, if not with him. What a beautiful touch.

The timing was extraordinary. We all have to go sometime, but it has become clear over the years that nobody gets to see anything through in this story. Mum passed away, waiting on Hindley's parole, which of course then dragged on right until her death. Hindley was about to file in Europe under new legislation, but she too never saw the daylight and now Winnie was deprived the moment that decades of mental strength had brought her to the threshold of. She wouldn't have got to ask Brady anything. He would not have revealed the answers she wanted. But she would have had her *moment* – like Mum was able to do – to rise above that mental control that he had placed on his victims and their families forever and a day.

And still the story rumbled on.

Just the previous year, in a bizarre twist, a woman was arrested in Carmarthanshire, on suspicion of preventing the lawful burial of a body. It is perhaps the only time you have heard of such a case and maybe not a significant crime – until it happens to involve you and Brady is involved.

Jackie Powell had been his mental health advocate in 1999 and the police had been informed that Brady had given her a letter for Winnie and on the envelope it read 'not to be opened until after [my] death'.

But the police found nothing by way of correspondence from Brady. Winnie's hopes and frustrations had grown again. Who knew what would actually emerge when the day finally came for *him* to meet his maker?

What happened in 2013 is proof that this never stops. The cycle that begun on that awful Boxing Day comes full circle in many aspects. We live with the pain on a daily basis, but some of the individuals who have wandered into our lives as a result disappear and then re-appear, making everything a whole lot worse, so there is no escape.

Caz Telfer had done her damage to our family, but the court now ruled that she had also done her time. In March 2013 she was released and was now finally Caron Foley. That meant that we began looking over our shoulder again, even though she was banned from the South of Manchester or from contacting any of our family. But we all knew the first aspect was hard to police and that, as history showed, you only had to be in touch once to cause maximum distraction.

As was the way now, she had complained about her human rights being abused. Hindley had used the same. The ability to play the system seemed to be at the expense of the victim. The parole board seemed duped into now thinking that she had finally admitted her crimes, but ignored the fact that she had shown no remorse whatsoever the previous year when there had been no grounds for them to release her.

I don't know where she is to this day. Sometimes you might pass someone in the street and wonder. If you see a fire, your mind goes back. An unrecognised number calling you and you might be momentarily concerned.

This is the knock on effect of Lesley being abducted, of being with Alan, of him befriending Telfer and Telfer killing my brother and niece. There is no respite. Melancholic and self-pitying it may sound, but you do often sit there – still, and wonder why and how.

And now just a couple of months after Telfer was free, Brady – where it all started – was appearing in public for the first time in nearly 50 years....

Those who said it should be held in private were probably correct. It became a show, not a mental health hearing. Brady denied insanity, but said that he killed for 'the existential experience'. What that really means is he wanted to sample what it was like, to discover how his mind might develop and what places it would take him to if he were to kill. It was a calculated thought process and self-serving. Death and murder were an opportunity to expand and explore his own brain.

You could probably therefore argue he was insane and mentally unwell. Equally, he had thought it through so thoroughly and on a level nobody else had really ever done, that in fact he was very well, extremely capable and beyond intelligence. The mental health ticket enabled you to play all sorts of cards – to your advantage and whenever it suited. Now, he was trying to engineer a move to Scotland and commence the re-writing of his own legacy. So the stories of steaks with the Krays were intertwined with details of his crimes. He recalled being a prison barber – as if you would want Brady cutting your hair. Your throat might be next. He toyed too with the notion that he might wish to commit suicide. On the one hand, he claimed the press tried to demonise him into some Jack the Ripper character – on the other he had big fantasies of his own portrayal.

He delivered for four hours, wavering from self-importance to cold-blooded killer. He tore into politicians, worshiping Labour's Roy Jenkins and slaughtering both Margaret Thatcher, who had made him a political prisoner, and Tony Blair whom he accused of getting rich off his war crimes.

In cross-examination, he was pedantic and sometimes mocking. He was convinced that the public's fascination with him was as strong as ever.

Most importantly – not once he did show remorse.

Terry Kilbride, who had probably become the most vocal of the 'group' in recent years watched from a separate courtroom, then branded the tribunal a waste of money. The nature of its public airing and all that brought racked up a bill of £250,000. All of us knew that the funds for providing platforms and legal challenges were limitless for Brady and Hindley. Yet, for the victims' families, that level of support did not ever exist. Sagely, Terry left the media with his own soundbite, recognising that it was the Ian Brady show – that money could have been used to find Keith's body.

There was some good news though. It emerged that Brady had been bed-ridden for two years and was probably terminally ill, suffering from emphysema and needed oxygen and a nebuliser four times a day.

And Brady's hearing failed. He was to remain at Ashworth – Terry Kilbride wanted him alive as long as possible in the hope that he might take us to Keith. Winnie's lawyer underlined that he had deprived children of their right to grow up and make decisions. He had no right, therefore, to decide his own fate.

The trial lasted eight days. His bid to be transferred refused left everybody wondering what the point had been. Through years of legalese, most of the challenges from Brady and Hindley had been knocked back. It left you with a double sensation. You were relieved that justice was done and that newer, younger politicians and decision-makers had not allowed time to cloud judgement and that was massive as the years rolled by, with all sorts of prisoners quoting human rights and European legislation. But also, it placed the families under enormous continuous stress, which then left us all asking what the cost and the amount of time had been for.

Furthermore, every time there was a new hearing or appeal, we suffer from the latest rhetoric. Brady describing his killings as 'recreational activities' and himself as a 'petty thief' were at odds with the gangster he described in Scotland and the Big Time Charlie who cooked with the Krays. They, of course, made us angry all over again, causing hurt with his language as if it were 1964 once more. This is the language that chips away at your brain, soul and day to day existence. It had been 49 years, but the tone and demeanour remained the same – and that made it worse, because of the absence of remorse. Equally, when there had been supposed confessions from Hindley you dismissed that too as a game for her own end.

The only benefit you could see in these proceedings dragging on was that the duration underlined the importance of the verdict and the airing of the facts often bought the case to a new audience, who were dealing with different atrocities on a different scale, like 9/11 and 7/7. Latter generations had simply grown up with murder on a more dramatic scale. Whilst Brady could get a lot of airtime from a public hearing, it also gave context to today's generation and that really was part of Mum's ethos that nobody would ever forget.

The hearing brought us nothing new. It was a cost-ridden showcase, but we were all left with one over-riding thought. Brady was definitely going to die soon, and all of us who remained would out-live him. That was the smallest, but sweetest of moral victories.

Chapter 37

In 2016, Alan passed away. That just left me in the family as the sole surviving member from that day. Mum, Brett and Tommy had all gone – and now Alan would join them.

He died after a blood clot following a fall. The press reported that he had fought a long battle against Parkinson's Disease. I think he had been hanging on for some time, and whatever you read into the Caz Telfer incident, and 'relationship' that was then and very likely naïve or he fell under a spell, the facts remain that he was there as a pivotal part of my life when Lesley went missing and, of course, whatever state Mum awoke in or whatever bad news came knocking at the door, for the duration of her life, he was always there too.

So, bar myself there was nobody now. The last family member was deceased. He was 81. In a final interview before he died, he had told the press that the memories of that day still haunted him and that he wouldn't rest until Brady was dead.

Yet, Brady had out-lived another one of us. This time it really hit home and it did so because of the fact that it was just me still standing.

I had rarely given an interview, let alone a quote, but somehow now felt compelled to do so. I was not box office TV, far from happy with the spotlight and the process, but there was nobody else now. It was up to me.

I told the reporter that it was just a joke…an absolute joke…that Brady was still alive and torturing people when everyone else was dead. And there is that double-edged sword again. Alan had a right to die at 81 through Parkinson's, but the fact that Brady survived him and everybody else makes you attribute their deaths to him – as though he is still winning, always controlling and ticking off one by one the obstacles in his way. Alan's death was perfectly logical and natural at that age in life, but it left a bitter taste because Brady was still there. We had begun to measure only in one context. Was the life shorter or longer than Brady's? Despite a lifetime of anxiety and stress and often a muted existence, I took a good look at myself in the mirror. I knew it would not be long. The hearing had pretty much said that Brady was on his way. I had to see this through.

It was a waiting game now. You couldn't wake up every morning and begin your day, asking the question, 'has he gone yet?'…yet at night you *would* go to bed thinking for the first time in years that he had survived another day. Alan's death really was a line in the sand.

Equally, if you turned on the now plentiful crime channels or TV news, still stories remained. They were getting less and less, but you only had to flick through those high numbers on the satellite channels and you would always find something about the Moors Murders.

I think I knew though that we were entering the final chapter…

* * *

It is May 16, 2017. It has been 53 years. My wife Linda is chatting on Facebook to Michelle, Terry Kilbride's partner. Two things that we took for granted across different eras met head on – going to a fair on Boxing Day in 1964 and social media today. Television was still really in its infancy when Lesley went missing. Now, we were all connected in one way or another. This was an unimaginable world back then.

'He hasn't got long,' Michelle typed to Linda.

Very soon after, she added more.

'He's gone. He's dead.'

'Has it been on TV yet?' Linda knew that then the floodgates would open and it would all begin again – for the final time.

And remember, my Linda inherited all this.

Michelle said it hadn't and that they were waiting to hear from the police.

They knew this day was coming and whatever plans and discretion they had already probably went out of the window. If Michelle and Linda were chatting online about it, the chances are so was someone else. Anyone at Ashworth or a police officer on his way home – any of them, despite what they are told not to discuss, would be hard pushed to get home and not say 'you will never guess what has happened…'

The clock was ticking inside authority. They needed to keep a lid on it for as long as possible to control the inevitable frenzy outside it. It would open intense media debate and we would all back there in 1964.

I never drunk at home, but pulled out a bottle of wine I had been saving. I didn't need to keep a lid on that.

I was quite possibly tipsy on the first sip. However seasoned a drinker you may or may not be, take an overdose of emotion, and small amounts of alcohol become lethal cocktails. The relief was total. I had come off so many nightshifts hoping to turn the radio on in the morning and hear the news, even though I knew that was unlikely as the police would without doubt have called us. But now that day was here.

I had done it. I had out-lived my sister's killer when nobody else had, and even though so many members of my family's passings had just augmented the resentment, I felt that I had stayed on for all of them and outlasting *him* was for everybody.

He wouldn't have the last laugh. That would be mine and tonight would last forever. I had no words, but a beaming smile, mixed with a river of teardrops. I was incontrollable between the two emotions – ecstatic that it was all over, devastated again that we had all been robbed of *many* lives and so much quality of life for no reason.

In an instant, I felt my heartbeat raise and my anxiety swell and, with the drink, disappear to a calmness, which I had not known since early childhood. And when the police finally called around 9 pm, I was probably more than a little merry.

Once they had rung, the phone didn't stop all night...I had been waiting for this day for so long. So very, very long. It is wrong to take pleasure in somebody else's death or indeed anticipate it so greatly, but this was so many years in the making and I literally did dance for joy. This is the supposed closure they talk about. There was never any bringing Lesley back, of course, but I came from 'an eye for an eye' generation and to see him outlive so many and deprive so many more of a quality of life at all – meant that, on this occasion I ask you to allow me to forsake manners and the rules of society for they were broken that Boxing Day.

I was absolutely ecstatic at his demise.

When I grew up we scrapped it out on the streets. That was the law of the land. Nobody called the cops. Now, everybody rings somebody if they disagree about something. We had come a long way – in the wrong direction. So, people handing out their own justice in their neighbourhood was a tolerance I bore and could accept. Nobody can deal with random targeting and when it is against a child of course the odds are stacked from the start and you never lose sight of that imbalance. It is not man to man stuff on the streets. It is controlling cowardice of a bully and psychopath – and with Brady's passing, I think when the news settled and reflections began, they were not for the brutal slaughtering of Lesley. I had – as you never do – sort of come to terms with that. They were for finally the measurement.

That means the size of all that we had lost. Lesley, and all the time that never happened. All the lost birthdays and Christmasses...all the shared moments of nothingness, like running in a field or nicking sweets from the shop...then the big stuff like exams, an eighteenth, leaving home, boyfriends and marriage, nieces and nephews, cars and fashions, shared moments in front of the TV that we would always remember, but meant nothing really, together with collective experiences from Mum's passing away to events in the national collective that everybody remembered, from the Queen's Jubilee in 1977

240

to Diana's death. At all these future moments that we were deprived from, there was always an empty seat.

Then there was consequence. There is absolutely no doubt that some of Brett and Charlene's issues would have been avoided if I had not walked with a glaze through my teens and into marriage, thinking it was a safety net when in fact, I was not ready and that just created more problems. This was a consequence of Boxing Day.

There is no doubt that my brother Tommy and my niece Kimberley would be alive today – bar ill health or a freak tragedy – if they had not been…the victims of a freak tragedy. That was a consequence of Boxing Day.

Equally, if I had found some strength and health when I was laid low with flu, and actually taken Les to the fair then my sister would be alive and probably none of this would have happened to our family.

That was Boxing Day. This is consequence.

So, Brady's death was met with immense delight – or relief – or anything you want. But, of course, it then led to this reflection about the waste – and that is all you can call it. He might have had his existentialist experience, but what purpose did any of this serve? Do you think that he thought for a second about the million moments he deprived of us. All the letters he wrote to Mum, trying to explain himself, but also playing a game of correction where he used her to adjust misrepresentation in the media, did he once weigh up our void?

No – it was all self-serving. Mum hoped to engineer certain outcomes from her correspondence that might answer or heal or provide fresh information, such as the whereabouts of Keith, but for Brady there was never forgiveness, nor a concept of what Lesley might be now.

Think how hard it is to celebrate a birthday or a Christmas, knowing that you are here and she is not and that her disappearance was Boxing Day. Imagine all the dark Christmases we have had.

Then you come to those landmarks in Lesley's life that you are left to – not so much half-celebrate – as just about acknowledge. And then what do you do? In the early years, it was impossible. In the latter years, you had learned to deal with it as numbness fell upon you, from the evening before to the morning after. Those people at football stadia who, instead of mourning a loss, clap and celebrate a life, are all very admirable for somebody they didn't know and are paying respects to.

We did know Lesley, but there wasn't enough life to celebrate.

So, we couldn't fake ourselves into some sort of party remembering her. The glazed sterile silence was the best we could offer. On birthdays and anniversaries, we would all withdraw within, keeping ourselves to ourselves with words at a premium. Applauding for a minute in a celebration of life is very decent, but if you are close to that person or within that family – as respectful as people are being – it is a farce, because all you want to do is shrink, hide and die within yourself. That is consequence.

A callous psychopathic murder for your own 'existential experience' – to (shall we say) see what it's like – bears no thought process for the people you leave behind, or the length of time that people will have to deal with it. In short, a lifetime. And there is no 'in short' about it. Because a lifetime is an eternity.

Think how many days we just stared out of the window. Imagine how when you think you are moving on and grasping contentment with Linda in my second marriage, or the times I spend with my children and grand-children, that actually I know that you cannot quite let yourself go. There is always something around the corner. The Moors Murders have been a circus for over 50 years.

Then there is the guilt that kicks in that just means you can never quite give it 100 % …if my kids or grandkids have ever seen me fully let go, be natural, seem without a care in the world, then I would be surprised. My sunken shoulders have rarely risen to full mast since that day.

You cannot ever know what lies in people's heads. Brett, younger than me, carried a brunt, and made life decisions accordingly. I probably would not have joined the Merchant Navy if this had not happened. He would not have gone to Germany. And then there is the next generation who pick up the pieces. Charlene, had a right to her own life and her own mind, but it was contaminated from day one by Mum feeding her, offloading on her and then stupidly blaming her. This was nothing to do with Chaz. This was consequence.

The kids and the grandkids had at least the right to be themselves, be free, and *be free* of this. Imagine being born into this world and dealt your cards and there are no aces to play. The kids just felt they had been given a losing hand and that, of course, descends into the next line of the family tree. That is consequence.

When people say the phrase 'today is the beginning of the rest of your life' they too mean it well, but they really can't, for the most part, understand the overtones of it. Invariably, they are being kind and supportive to someone who has hit a buffer.

I can tell you, that whilst I will never forget Lesley or move on, nor begrudge having a Mum in a fit state for much of my life, that day the call came in to say he was gone was – despite my years and all the chances to utter that phrase – the first time I could do so with sincerity. Closure, I am coming to meet you.

I missed Mum and Lesley every day and I missed them doubly when the news was confirmed. But, for the first time, his control had subsided and we had won. There were, of course, no trophies, to be claimed unlike his desire at every moment and every junction.

Closure? Not really. Moral victory – yes, for me in that I had survived him. A chance to find the beginning of the rest of my life?

My God, I hoped so…

Chapter 38

But first the circus rolled into town. The ending of an era only served to re-invent the story. Plus, there was the phony war of double bluff, 'fake news' and protocol. I knew that media interest would peak again. This was the end of their story too. The feeding frenzy was over. All that was left realistically was for people to come forward who had never done so, Brady's lawyer to comment, media to speculate and the actual burial itself.

I know one thing. When I woke the morning after the news, I was still ecstatic. Of course, the phone continued to ring. Even though I didn't answer, it was obviously the press! Somebody would give them the quote they would need or they could just make it up like they had before. They didn't quite seem to understand however that whilst the mood was upbeat in my family, it remained a private moment and that reflection was for Lesley – and Mum, and therefore Tommy and Kimberely. We grieved a little too, but not at his demise, rather at all those memories we never had. So, we were sad and therefore the media were an intrusion on our grief, but my goodness, we really did feel it was over.

Except, of course, there was a little more to come. Charlene said to me, with years of understanding under her belt, 'You know what is going to happen now'.

And she was right. Another circus would follow. For now, we were exhausted and we hadn't even done anything. I am no great expert on the human condition, but the sheer fatigue that we felt within minutes of the news coming through must be a fifty-year-old tension that had nowhere to go within the body, that it supressed itself and finally only now found its outlet. It is fair to say though that one thing had not changed – my guilt remained.

The day after the inquest (some four moths later), Keith Bennett's family hit the news – they were demanding Brady's famous suitcases be opened. You may recall Brady and the suitcases. There were two of them, believed to be in the hands of his lawyer. Keith's family thought they might hold clues as to his whereabouts. Brady had insisted just days before his death that they remain locked. I think you have to assume that there was stuff in there that he wanted to literally take to the grave to him. He had so little family sentimentality and had spent so long inside that you surely conclude that he wanted to play the game a little more after his death. Was this another existential outing for him? Torment and control remained his weapons. Winnie had an argument for keeping him alive in the hope, the faintest of beliefs that one day he might provide the answers. She had preceded him in death. The answers more than likely followed him to his grave.

That itself remained a mystery. There were already numerous stories that no undertaker in Manchester would bury him, as with Hindley. I find that hard to believe. Most people's business cynicism overrides their ethics and somebody surely – just like his lawyer defending him – would have seen some benefit in being the company that took him to his final destination.

There was talk too that his body lay waiting in a morgue next to Salmon Abedi, the bomber of the Manchester Arena a month after. Nobody would go near the pair of them. Leave them be. I am sure both had a lot to talk about.

That measures the passage of time. One of the most atrocious killers from yesterday meets headlong today's most notorious. Two individuals who had carried out despicable crimes with devastating consequences were now, if the stories were true, lying on a cold abandoned slab, with just each other for company.

The inquest itself found pneumonia as a cause…and heart failure. I am tempted to suggest they must have done well to find the heart. The coroner ordered that Brady's ashes should not be scattered at Saddleworth. Apparently his human rights could have allowed that. He concluded that he was a sexual deviant with massive interest in paedophilia, and that in effect the hunger strike was all a sham and that Brady had regularly received full meals from 'selected staff' at all times. He was not emaciated. So, that meant he was playing the public and had been the courts for many years with this hunger strike nonsense. Confirmed. Frankly, I did wonder how he could survive so long with nothing inside him. Now, I know why. It was inaccurate.

By October 2017, a judge had ruled that the responsibility for Brady's body no longer remained with the solicitor, that he should not be given a burial and that no music be played at the disposal of his remains. The issue had been forced by Tameside and Oldham Councils, who had expressed concern that five months on he had still not been buried, after getting wind of a whisper that the solicitor had indeed intended Saddleworth as the home for his ashes! This was denied, but still, Brady's legal team would not reveal their hand as to where a 'burial' might take place. The judge concluded that matters had gone on long enough and the matter needed to be closed.

Yes it did – even he was seeking that closure.

We were starting to hear murmurs of the likely outcome well in advance of the public. The desperate need to control this information was paramount. It only took one lone crazy individual to somehow make this about them and the whole thing would be a shambles.

By early November, what we were told to be true appeared to be confirmed. That Brady's ashes had been taken from a crematorium in Southport near Liverpool and scattered at sea. The ceremony had taken place without fanfare and outside of hours to avoid distress to other families on that day. Who had the job of casting such misery into the ocean, I do not know. They set sail out of Liverpool Marina after two in the morning. You would like to think that Brady succumbed to a tempestuous night of mountain-high waves, thrown to the wolves as a gale bashed the shore. But it didn't really matter. Like Keith, he had no grave. There was no martyr site for Moors Murders obsessives to visit in their misguided stupidity.

That ship had sailed, Caz Telfer. Nobody would ever know and that should be the end of the story.

Almost one year on I write this. I do have a level of stability and tranquillity that should remain with me until the day I die. There is little left to say. From time to time there will be other stories or documentaries made. Another anniversary will pop up and briefly we will go back there again. In February 2019, Mum would have been dead 20 years and by September reached 90. My goodness me, she would have loved to have outlived Brady. That remained my prerogative and he was gone now, leaving me with the rest of my life finally ahead of me and a backdrop of shattered dreams, intolerable flashbacks and damaged relationships – plus the loss of my brothers and niece and serious doubts over the man who brought me up, Alan West.

I am old and enough and wise enough to understand that Lesley went to the fair and walked into the path of two deadly psychopaths. What then happened remains shocking today. The audio tapes – aired just once or twice – are graphic enough to induce vomit and inspire anybody older to offer themselves to take that pain and brutal mutilation for themselves in place of a child.

I, of course, put her in that position by not going to the fair. I see the sixty-something man in the mirror and the mental scars of pain look back at me. I know well enough that a lifetime of anxiety is the price for a handful of hours of torture that Lesley had to endure.

Oh to be poorly again at Christmas. Every time I feel run down or flu-like, I know I can fight it until my own time is up. Nothing can be that debilitating that it leaves you bed-ridden as it did on that Boxing Day. If I had known the mental anguish that would have ensued when a ten year old did not go to the fair, I would have found strength in those legs to rise from the couch and Lesley would be with us today, and all of our lives would have come to that fork in the road and headed in a different direction, without any overflow to the next generation.

It has been so difficult to get this out of my system. It has been a lifetime's work. I still blame myself. I know it could have been so different.

I wish I had gone to the fair.

If only.